Cuba
socialism &
democracy

**Debates on the Revolution
and Cuba Today**

by Peter Taaffe

CWI Publications 2000

Cuba: Socialism & Democracy -
Debates on the Revolution and Cuba Today
by Peter Taaffe
© CWI Publications 2000

First Edition June 2000
Classification:
Peter Taaffe
Cuba: Socialism & Democracy - Debates on the Revolution and Cuba Today
Politics/Economics/History

ISBN 1-870958225 pbk

A catalogue record for this book is available
from the British Library

Published by Socialist Books (formerly Fortress Books)
for The Committee for a Workers' International
Designed and typeset by Kavita Graphics (TU)
Typeset in Usherwood 9 pt
Printed by Biddles Ltd of Guildford and Kings Lynn
Printed on 100% wood-free paper

Distribution by Socialist Books
PO Box 24697, London, E11 1YD
Telephone +44 (0)20 8988 8789

cover photo: Fidel Castro & Che Guevara, Havana 1959
cover design: Kavita Graphics +44 (0)20 8533 9989

Cuba
socialism & democracy

Acknowledgments

I wish to thank the following individuals for their efforts in helping to ensure this book was published: Kevin Parslow and Manny Thain in typing the manuscript. Kevin Parslow deserves a special mention for his unflagging efforts in assembling important documents and his famous attention to detail. Lynn Walsh, as always, provided invaluable suggestions and criticisms as did Tony Saunois, Hannah Sell, Clare Doyle, Bob Labi, Per Olsson, Simon Kaplan, Ken Smith and Steve Jolly. Annoesjka Valent also brought to my attention some important source material. Lastly, I would like to thank Dennis Rudd for his layout skills and Mick Cotter for arranging the printing of this book.

About the Author

Peter Taaffe is the General Secretary of the Socialist Party, the section of the Committee for a Workers' International in England and Wales, and a member of the CWI's International Secretariat. From 1964 he was Editor of Militant, the Marxists inside the Labour Party. Increasing support for Marxist ideas in the Labour Party led to its National Executive Committee expelling him in 1983, along with the four other members of the Militant Editorial Board.

Following the magnificent struggle of the Liverpool labour movement in the mid-1980s and the expulsion of the leading supporters of Militant on Merseyside, and the mighty anti-poll tax struggle led by Militant, opposed viciously by the Labour leaders, the majority of Militant supporters formed Scottish Militant Labour in 1992 and Militant Labour in England and Wales a year later. Peter has been General Secretary of firstly Militant Labour from 1993, and following its change of name in 1997, of the Socialist Party.

Peter has been the author of three books: Liverpool: the City That Dared to Fight (with Tony Mulhearn), published in 1988, The Masses Arise, in 1989, about the French Revolution, both published by Fortress Books, and The Rise of Militant, in 1995, by Militant Publications. He has also written innumerable pamphlets and articles, particularly for The Socialist and Socialism Today and their predecessors Militant and Militant International Review.

Introduction

The Cuban Revolution triumphed in 1959, more than four decades ago. Yet, its effects, particularly through its most charismatic figures, Fidel Castro and the murdered Che Guevara, still inspire workers and young people worldwide. The overthrow of the hated dictatorship of Batista was quickly followed by the elimination of landlordism and capitalism. The world labour movement was mesmerised by this. A government and a 'socialist' regime had been established in the very 'jaws of the monster', US imperialism. Writers and commentators drew parallels with previous revolutions, particularly the Russian Revolution. However, history never repeats itself in exactly the same way. Nor do revolutions. The Cuban Revolution was entirely different to the Russian Revolution, in its origins, the political outlook of its leading figures and the class forces involved.

Indeed, nothing in the socialist and Marxist textbooks – of Marx, Engels, Lenin, Luxemburg or even Trotsky – fully prepared Marxists for what happened in Cuba. It is true that in his last writings, Trotsky gave some indication of processes which later developed in the Cuban Revolution. He pointed out that leaders from a non-Marxist middle-class background could, in conditions of extreme social crisis, be pushed much further than they originally intended and into breaking with capitalism. The British Marxists also, who later published the newspaper Militant (now The Socialist, weekly paper of the Socialist Party) were better prepared than most for the events of the Cuban Revolution. Their analysis of the Chinese Revolution of 1944-49 and the processes in the postwar period which unfolded in the neo-colonial world meant that they were not taken completely unawares by events in Cuba. Yet even the best theory is not able to fully anticipate how a revolution will actually unfold.

The Cuban Revolution was led by Castro and Guevara, and their 26 July Movement, which originated outside of the Stalinist tradition. They established a regime enjoying massive, overwhelming popular support and which evoked enthusiasm in Cuba itself and acclaim from the oppressed worldwide. In its first phase, moreover, the revolution evinced tendencies of mass involvement and participation, including elements of workers' control and of 'popular power'. This compelled every socialist and Marxist to assess the precise character of the Cuban regime. Could the government of Fidel Castro and Che Guevara be compared to that of Lenin, Trotsky and the Bolsheviks in the first heroic period of the Russian Revolution? A planned economy had been established but was there real workers' democracy in Cuba? What were the international dimensions and the effects of the

Cuban Revolution? These issues were hotly debated at the time, and have been a source of constant controversy since.

These are also the themes of this book, judged against the background of events since 1959. Many, including some claiming to be Marxists and Trotskyists, were, in our opinion, swept off their feet by the Cuban Revolution. They replaced a balanced Marxist appraisal – support for the revolution but linking this to proposals for establishing workers' democracy in Cuba – with impressionism. This did involve comparing the government and the state in Cuba to that of the Bolsheviks in the first period after 1917. We opposed this and from the very outset of the revolution attempted to give an all-sided analysis and explanation that could prepare workers for the subsequent developments in Cuba and particularly the Cuban state.

Our ideas were presented in our weekly newspaper Militant and in other publications. I wrote three articles for our newspaper in 1978, which were subsequently gathered together and published as a small pamphlet. I have included this pamphlet as an appendix. This provides important background information on the events leading up to the revolution of 1959 and afterwards. Readers can also, if they wish, read our original analysis in the light of subsequent criticisms.

Twenty-one years later Doug Lorimer, one of the leaders of the Australian-based Democratic Socialist Party decided to subject this pamphlet to a lengthy criticism. This book is a reply to these criticisms. However, before we received Lorimer's criticisms I already had the intention of writing an up-to-date analysis of the situation in Cuba today which would involve a revisiting of the events of the Cuban Revolution itself.

The topicality of such a work has been underlined recently by the worldwide publicity around the Cuban boy Elian Gonzalez, which has once more brought Cuba back to the centre of world politics. The outcome of this conflict, with the 'capture' of Elian by the INS, which led to him being reunited with his father, represented a defeat for the die-hard ultra-right Miami exiles. At the same time, it has drawn attention once more to Fidel Castro's government and political regime, and to the future prospects for the development of Cuba itself.

In this book we touch on some of the main current developments in Cuba but a substantial work, giving a more detailed overall picture of events in Cuba, I have had to put aside in order to reply to the arguments of the DSP with, we hope, some benefits to be gained. Discussion, criticisms and counter-criticisms of different trends within the workers' movement and amongst Marxists can serve to clarify and educate a new generation who are not yet familiar with our analysis.

I have felt it necessary to reply to the DSP, in the order in which they have set out their criticisms of my pamphlet. This necessarily involves a certain sacrifice of style and presentation in order to properly deal with these arguments. There are also quite lengthy quotes from different authors and publications, which is necessary because of disputes over facts. I hope this is not too burdensome for the reader but will, on the contrary, serve to illuminate and underline the analysis which we have made of the Cuban Revolution, the character of Fidel Castro and his government, and the present and future perspectives for Cuba, which are of vital concern for workers everywhere.

Peter Taaffe
May 2000

Sugercane workers, Cuba, 1988.

Cuba Today

The collapse of the Berlin Wall ten years ago led not just to the elimination of the odious political regimes of Stalinism in Eastern Europe and the former Soviet Union, but also the last vestiges of the planned economies which were the economic base of these societies. The economic counter-revolution brought in its wake unprecedented hardship and suffering for the mass of the population in these countries. Consequently capitalism appeared to reign supreme throughout the planet with the 'market' presented as the only viable economic system for humankind. The massive pro-market ideological campaign sought to bury socialism and the ideas of the socialist transformation of society once and for all.

However, a few regimes, Cuba most prominently amongst them, have seemingly held out against the tide of social counter-revolution. For this reason, together with the considerable historical and social achievements of the revolution and the partial recovery of the economy recently, Cuba seems to be a symbol of hope, particularly for those among the younger generation who are rediscovering socialist and Marxist ideas. It appears to be a continued vindication of the socialist project. Yet in the early 1990s in the wake of the collapse in the former USSR and Eastern Europe, Cuba itself was on the knife-edge. Its economic lifeline was the market of the USSR in particular for its main export of sugar, coupled with huge subsidies it received from the same quarter. This was abruptly cut off as the pro-capitalist wing of the bureaucracy in the USSR and Eastern Europe stole state industry and transformed these societies into capitalist states. Under the pressure of world capitalism, their new friends, they spitefully and precipitately cut Cuba's economic lifeline.

This was to have terrible economic and social consequences for the people of Cuba. Through COMECON, the trading bloc of the former USSR and Eastern Europe, the policy of selling oil (from the USSR) for sugar (from Cuba) and other subsidies was worth a huge $5 billion annually to Cuba.[1] This was now drastically cut and the Cuban government was compelled to introduce rationing of food and fuel consumption. Fidel Castro himself declared that the action of Cuba's former 'Communist' allies was 'repugnant' and that moreover they would *"have blood on their hands in the event of a [US] invasion"*.[2] In April 1991 Castro declared that a total of 85 per cent of Cuba's foreign trade *"had crumbled in a matter of months"*.[3] The collapse of COMECON had also reduced imports into Cuba by over 80 per cent and the 'global social product' of the economy had plummeted by 25 per cent in 1991.[4]

US capitalism, seeking to profit from this, enacted the 1992 Torricelli Bill and the Helms-Burton Act of 1996 to further cripple the Cuban economy. It even outlawed overseas subsidiaries of US firms from trading with Cuba. The cumulative effect of over 40 years of US sanctions has resulted in Cuba losing a total of US$40 billion, *"far in excess of any damage done to the US economy through the Cuban expropriation of US property".*[5] Nevertheless, in the latter part of the 1990s even in this besieged fortress, Cuba managed to painfully crawl out of the economic abyss. By 1994 there was economic growth of 0.7 per cent, 2.5 percent in 1995, and 7.8 per cent growth in 1996, with a drop in 1997, but a small recovery in subsequent years. This contrasts favourably with the collapse in the former USSR and Eastern Europe. In the case of the former the drop in production is the greatest ever in history, an even sharper plunge than that caused by the 1929-33 world capitalist slump. Part of the explanation for Cuba's growth is the significant rise in income from tourism. Cuba now has more tourist beds than the rest of the Caribbean put together. But it is also the result of the maintenance of a planned economy, despite the absence of workers' democracy, which has allowed Cuba to at least maintain itself despite facing monumental difficulties.

Moreover, its performance in health, education, pensions and welfare generally has been outstanding, particularly when set against the background of the conditions of the masses in neighbouring Central and South America. Primary and preventative healthcare has meant that Cuba has an infant mortality rate half of Washington, DC's! There have been spectacular developments in eye surgery, which has attracted visitors from all over the world. And despite the chronic shortages of medicines and equipment, Cuba's health services stand out as a beacon for the masses in the Caribbean and Latin America. Thousands of doctors and nurses trained in Cuba work in Central America and Haiti. Castro boasted: *"We will produce better doctors than in the United States."*[6]

The very viciousness of the American embargo has compelled Cuba to fall back on its own resources: *"We all became inventors; there was no alternative,"* declared Doctor Aleida Guevara (daughter of Che).[7] As a result of the development of Cuba's biotechnology industry it has pioneered a vaccine against meningitis which is in demand internationally. And while the poor have undoubtedly suffered because of the US-led embargo nevertheless, as The Guardian put it in 1998:

"In terms of accessing those basic attributes of a humane society Cuba scores very highly. In the most recent index set out in the 1997 Human Development Report, Cuba is in the top group of five developing countries which have reduced human poverty to the point at which it affects less than 10 per cent of the population. Cuba's performance is above Costa Rica and way above that of Jamaica, El Salvador and Haiti." [8]

All of this demonstrates the great advantages of a planned economy, even one hamstrung by a top-heavy bureaucracy, compared to outmoded capitalism. Cuba's longevity rate is 75 years, fully 20 years more than in the collapsing, catastrophic former USSR.

Moreover, Fidel Castro himself, unlike the ex-bureaucrats Gorbachev, Yeltsin, etc, has not rushed to embrace the market. In words he still defends 'socialism' as an alternative to capitalism, although in Cuba itself he has been compelled to make big concessions to the market as the price for his government's continued existence. It is for these reasons that Cuba has earned the sympathy and support of socialists and even Marxists. There is also a renewed interest in the Cuban Revolution and its relevance to the struggle for world socialism. The Socialist Party in Britain (formerly Militant) and the Committee for a Workers' International (CWI) have always implacably defended the gains of the Cuban Revolution, while criticising the political regime of Castro and the Communist Party of Cuba. We demand an immediate end to the embargo against Cuba. Others, some claiming to be Marxists and Trotskyists, have closed their eyes to the absence of workers' democracy in Cuba. One such organisation is the Australian-based Democratic Socialist Party (DSP).

The DSP on Nicaragua and Afghanistan

Seeking to capitalise on the undoubted sympathy for the achievements of the Cuban revolution, the leaders of this organisation act as uncritical cheerleaders for Fidel Castro, his policies and his regime. There is nothing new or distinct in this approach of the DSP leadership. This organisation is nothing if not consistent. They uncritically supported the Sandanista leadership during the Nicaraguan revolution, which ultimately led to their break with Trotskyism.

"The Nicaraguan Revolution of 1979 was decisive in shifting our perspectives. The Nicaraguan Revolution toppled our Trotskyist theory that socialist revolutions were one-stage affairs, and vindicated the two-stage strategy of revolution developed by Lenin." [9]

We will say more later about Lenin's alleged "two-stage" strategy. But it is undeniable that the Nicaraguan Revolution stalled and was eventually rolled back because of the incorrect policies and methods of the Sandanista leadership. Thus the DSP abandoned a correct idea, the permanent revolution, for policies – the two-stage idea – which were responsible for derailing a revolution. They also supported the Russian Stalinist invasion of Afghanistan in 1979-80:

"The Soviet intervention in Afghanistan in December 1979 was another world event that forced us to think things out more for ourselves (sic)...Soviet troops went in to

Afghanistan to block a US-organised war to topple a radical regime in Kabul. Our response was prompt – to give strong support to the Soviet and Kabul government forces in the Afghan civil war." [10]

It was entirely wrong, even 'critically', for Marxists to support the intervention of the Stalinist regime of the USSR in Afghanistan in 1979. The fact that this action propped up the Afghan regime which did carry through important progressive measures in land reform, abolition of the bride price etc, was secondary for the Stalinists in the USSR in furthering their own strategic interests in the region. For this reason we opposed the initial decision to intervene in Afghanistan, which contrary to the arguments of the DSP, allowed imperialism a propaganda victory in identifying 'socialism' with bureaucratic-military means to extend the Soviet elite's sphere of influence. On the other hand we opposed those who then demanded the immediate withdrawal of Russian troops, which concretely would have led many years earlier to the installation of a regime on the lines of the monstrous fundamentalist Taliban government that rules today.

The DSP were also uncritical cheerleaders for Gorbachev, gatekeeper for the social counter-revolution in the former Soviet Union, even printing and sporting T-shirts with Gorbachev's image on them. Abandoning the idea of a political revolution – a regime of workers' democracy – made by the masses in the Stalinist states, the DSP transferred their hopes for 'democratisation' to the summits of the Russian bureaucracy:

"Even before the coming to power of Mikhail Gorbachev, we [the DSP] had started to leave open the possibility that the process of democratic reform in these countries might actually be initiated from within the ruling Communist Party." [11]

At a time of utmost peril for the Cuban Revolution in the early 1990s, Gorbachev, at the bidding of US imperialism, withdrew Russian troops and military personnel. The Cuban CP newspaper 'Granma' declared that this had given the "green light to a US invasion". The Socialist Party and the CWI, unlike the DSP, never **once** supported this ally of US imperialism who opened the way for Yeltsin's restoration of capitalism in the USSR and attempted to choke Cuba to death.

In the neo-colonial world the DSP is uncritical, not to say sycophantic, towards the leadership of left formations, reinforcing their theoretical and programmatic mistakes, and advancing a version of the Stalinist theory of 'stages' for the revolution in the neo-colonial world. They have explicitly rejected Trotsky's theory of the permanent revolution, both as an explanation of the motive forces of the Russian Revolution and, more importantly, its relevance today to the struggle unfolding in

Asia, Latin America and Africa. In Indonesia, their ideas, if they were to become the guiding principles of a mass workers' movement, would play a disastrous role in derailing the revolution which has just begun.

The DSP leadership are deepening and extending the mistakes made by the leadership of the United Secretariat of the Fourth International (USFI) throughout most of the post-1945 period. Incapable of building sizeable formations amongst the working class they invariably abandoned an independent Marxist analysis, and acted as political attorneys for 'radicals', Stalinists or leaders of the national liberation movements in the neo-colonial world. They developed a relatively uncritical position towards Mao Zedong, following the victory of the Chinese Revolution, with the majority of the USFI believing that a political revolution in China was unnecessary. They uncritically supported Tito in Yugoslav Stalinism's confrontation with the Stalinists in the USSR. In Vietnam they adopted a similarly uncritical position towards the National Liberation Front, with their main slogan on demonstrations against US imperialism's intervention being 'Ho, Ho, Ho Chi Minh', elevating the leader of the Stalinist state of North Vietnam into a hero. Militant (now the Socialist Party) implacably defended the struggle of the workers and peasants of South Vietnam and of the revolution. But we never uncritically supported the leaders of the NLF or Ho Chi Minh. The victory of the Vietnamese Revolution was a big step forward but because of the nationalist limitations of the leadership and the major forces involved in the struggle – largely a peasant army – the kind of state that would come out of the revolution we predicted would be a planned economy but with a one-party Stalinist regime. It was therefore necessary to warn workers in advance of the likely outcome of events. We also supported the Algerian Revolution in the late 1950s and early 1960s with political and material support in the war of national liberation against French imperialism. But at the same time we never gave uncritical support to the leadership of the NLF of Ben Bella, which the USFI did.

Because of the relative political quiescence of the working class, particularly during the long boom of the 1950s and 1960s, the USFI abandoned, in effect, the working class as the main agency of socialist revolution. Other forces – students in the 'red bases' in the universities, the radicalised peasantry and intelligentsia in the neo-colonial world, and 'reforming' Stalinist bureaucrats – were apportioned that role which by rights belongs to the organised working class. Marxism, from the time of Marx and Engels themselves, has based itself upon the working class not for romantic or secondary reasons but because of the role that this class plays in production and society. It is the only class, organised by big industry, which possesses the potential collective power and consciousness to carry through the socialist revolution. Other classes, the middle class or the peasantry for instance, are heterogeneous. They are divided into different layers, with an upper section looking towards the capitalists and the lower, poorer sections of the peasantry tending to merge with the working class. In the neo-colonial world the peasantry can play an auxiliary role in an alliance with the working class in the transformation of society but the main role, the leader of the socialist revolution, is the working class. The consequence of the USFI's abandonment of this basic tenet of Marxism was seen in 1968, which saw the greatest general strike in history involving ten million French workers. These putative 'leaders' of the working class were caught completely unawares. Historically they were found to be facing in the wrong direction, towards 'red bases' in the universities and not towards the working class.

Impatience and a desire to reap what has not already been sown by past support and influence, led much of the small forces of Trotskyism to search for classes other than the working class and other political forces to do the job which they were incapable of doing. The DSP originates from this tradition. However, they have gone further in tail-ending radical organisations and leaders in the third world and dignifying them with ideas that they don't have or glossing over theoretical mistakes and programmatic deficiencies, which could prove fatal for coming movements of the working class and poor peasantry.

This is clearly shown in an article attacking the Committee for a Workers' International's position on Cuba by Doug Lorimer, one of the leaders of the DSP.[12] He has subjected the leadership of the CWI to sustained criticism, the latest example of which is an attack on a pamphlet on the Cuban Revolution by Peter Taaffe, which he blandly calls a 'criticism'.

We confess that to be attacked by Lorimer and his particularly toothless brand of 'Marxism' is the equivalent of what the British politician Denis Healey characterised as being "savaged by a dead sheep". Normally it would be pointless to reply to such diatribes, which are ten a penny in Britain from every insignificant sect. They have never done anything worthwhile but grind their teeth in fruitless frustration at the achievements of Militant, which alone of the Trotskyist organisations in Western Europe managed on two occasions in Britain to establish a significant base in mass movements amongst working people: in the Liverpool struggle between 1983 and 1987, and in the mighty anti-poll tax struggle which humbled Thatcher and consigned her to political oblivion. We have also pursued successful mass work in a number of other countries: Ireland, Sweden, Sri Lanka, Nigeria, Austria, etc.

The purpose of Lorimer's 'article' (which runs to 25 A4 pages) is revealed right at the beginning:

"The following article was written at the request of Farooq Tariq, General Secretary of the Labour Party Pakistan, as an initial contribution to a discussion between the LPP and the DSP on the character of the leadership of the Cuban socialist state and the Communist Party of Cuba".[13]

Thus the DSP, it seems, has been pressed into service by Farooq Tariq to supply him with arguments that would allow him to distance himself from his previous position on Cuba, when he was a member of the CWI. He was excluded from the ranks of the CWI because his 'party' was nothing more than a front for a Non-Governmental Organisation (NGO), with subventions from the Swedish trade unions and social democrats, which operated on the basis of patronage and uncritical support for corrupt trade union leaders, rather than seeking to build an independent revolutionary party in Pakistan. The DSP are thus facilitating the political retreat of those like Farooq Tariq who, at least in words (although it is doubtful whether he fully understood the ideas) once put forward a principled, Trotskyist, Marxist approach towards the Cuban revolution.

The Permanent Revolution

The justification for a lengthy reply to the arguments advanced by them lies not in the importance of the DSP or of Farooq Tariq themselves. It flows from the need to reach and convince the leaders and ranks of more important organisations, which exist now and more importantly will arise in the neo-colonial world and elsewhere in the future, of a genuine Marxist method of analysis. The Cuban Revolution is not just of historical interest alone. The complicated and contradictory circumstances in which the Cuban Revolution took place have relevance to the situation that is developing in the neo-colonial world at the moment. In the stormy events in Venezuela and possibly in Ecuador too are to be found many of the features contained in the Cuban Revolution more than 40 years ago. Whether these countries or others take to the Cuban road, even whether it is possible to repeat in the modern context what happened in Cuba, is of burning topical importance for socialist and Marxist forces in Latin America at the moment. A misunderstanding of the real lessons of the Cuban Revolution could be fatal for the revolutionary forces today. It is therefore not pedantry, or an attempt at self-justification, which has led us to take up the arguments of the DSP leadership in relation to Cuba.

However, before dealing with the Cuban revolution as such it is necessary to give a brief outline of Trotsky's theory of the Permanent Revolution and its relevance today. This is particularly necessary in view of the DSP's criticisms of this theory both historically and its relevance to the Cuban revolution, and to the problems of the neo-colonial world today. DSP leader John Percy writes:

"Our errors flowed from the schema we had had – Trotsky's theory of permanent revolution." [14]

The DSP, as we have seen, confronted with what they considered was a "socialist revolution" in Nicaragua threw overboard Trotsky's celebrated Theory of the Permanent Revolution which correctly foreshadowed the class forces involved in the victory of the Russian Revolution and how the working class in October 1917 were victorious in setting up the first democratic workers' state in history. The most important law of the dialectic is 'truth is concrete'. This basic axiom of Marxism is foreign to Lorimer. In its place are empty historical abstractions without any attempt to deal with recent or past history. The leadership of the DSP now have some difficulty in explaining why the 'socialist revolution', which was conducted in Nicaragua under the signboard of 'two stages', led to defeat and the disintegration of the Sandanista movement. The ultimate test of theory is practice. If the Nicaraguan Revolution was sufficient reason for throwing overboard the Theory of Permanent Revolution by the DSP why has it not led to a break with landlordism and capitalism and the establishment of a workers' state in Nicaragua?

Lorimer not only fires a broadside at the Socialist Party but has also spent 78 pages in a recent pamphlet ("Trotsky's theory of Permanent Revolution: A Leninist critique") allegedly refuting Trotsky and yet there is not one mention as to how this applies to the post-1945 period or the current world situation. And this is not an accident. Because where Lorimer's ideas have been tried it has resulted in an aborted revolution, in Nicaragua. In the past, moreover, in every revolution or revolutionary situation where it was applied by the Stalinists and the latter-day converts to Stalinist theories such as the DSP, we saw the same result.

What is Trotsky's Theory of the Permanent Revolution and how much did it coincide with Lenin's pre-1917 ideas and where did it differ from them? The DSP are incapable of answering this question. Trotsky and Lenin, indeed the whole of Russian Marxism, were at one in seeing the main task of the Russian Revolution as the completion of the bourgeois-democratic revolution: elimination of feudal and semi-feudal relations in the land, unification of the country and the solution of the national question, democracy – the right to vote for a democratic parliament, a free press, trade union rights, etc – and the freeing of the economy from the domination of imperialism. Lenin and Trotsky differed from the Mensheviks who believed that the task of the working class was to tail end the liberal bourgeoisie who they consid-ered were the main agent of the bourgeois democratic revolution. Moreover they saw this as a necessary and inevitable stage of development for Russia without any serious international ramifications. However the belated development of the bourgeoisie as a class and the bourgeois-democratic revolution in Russia meant that they were incapable of completing this historic task. The capitalists invested in land and the landlords invested in industry. Therefore any thoroughgoing bourgeois democratic revolution would come up against the opposition not just of the landlords but of the bourgeoisie and their political representatives, the liberal bourgeois parties. They had demonstrated again and again not just in Russia, but in Germany in the nineteenth century and elsewhere that they were incapable of carrying their own revolution through to a conclusion.

The powerful and then unique development of the Russian proletariat, explained Trotsky, also affected the liberal bourgeoisie's preparedness to carry the revolution through. They were terrified, quite correctly as events demonstrated, that a struggle against the thousand-year old Tsarist regime and the social foundations upon which it rested would open the floodgates through which the working class, together with the peasantry, would pour and place on the agenda its own demands. Both Trotsky and Lenin agreed therefore that it was an alliance of the working class and the peasantry, the majority of the population of Russia, who were the only force capable of completing the bourgeois-democratic revolution. Where they differed was on the issue of who would exercise the leadership in this alliance. Would it be the working class or the peasantry? Moreover, once this alliance had come to power, who would be the dominant force in the government? Would it just carry through the bourgeois democratic revolution or would it be forced to go further?

Trotsky, in his Theory of the Permanent Revolution, argued that history attested to the fact that the peasantry had never played an independent role (as we explained above). It must be led by the one of the other two great classes in society: the bourgeoisie or the working class. However, Lenin and Trotsky agreed that the bourgeoisie could not carry through their own revolution. Therefore, argued Trotsky, the working class must assume the leadership of the revolution drawing behind it the masses in the countryside. In a very important summing up of the 'three conceptions of the Russian Revolution' in August 1939, a year before his assassination by the Stalinists, Trotsky makes the following comments about Lenin's formula of the 'democratic dictatorship of the proletariat and peasantry'. He states:

"Lenin's conception represented an enormous step forward in so far as it proceeded not from constitutional reforms but from the agrarian overturn as the central task of the revolution and singled out the only realistic combination of social forces for its accomplishment. The weak point of Lenin's conception, however, was the internally contradictory idea of 'the democratic dictatorship of the proletariat and peasantry'. Lenin himself underscored the fundamental limitation of this 'dictatorship' when he

*openly called it **bourgeois**. By this he meant to say that for the sake of preserving its alliance with the peasantry the proletariat would in the coming revolution have to forego the direct posing of the socialist tasks. But this would signify the renunciation by the proletariat of its **own** dictatorship. Consequently, the gist of the matter involved the dictatorship of the peasantry even if with the participation of the workers."* [15]

But then Trotsky goes on to comment:

"The peasantry is dispersed over the surface of an enormous country whose key junctions are the cities. The peasantry itself is incapable of even formulating its own interests inasmuch as in each district these appear differently. The economic link between the provinces is created by the market and the railways, but both the market and the railways are in the hands of the cities. In seeking to tear itself away from the restrictions of the village and to generalise its own interests, the peasantry inescapably falls into political dependence upon the city. Finally, the peasantry is heterogeneous in its social relations as well: the kulak stratum [rich peasants] naturally seeks to swing it to an alliance with the urban bourgeoisie while the nether strata of the village pull to the side of the urban workers. Under these conditions the peasantry as such is completely incapable of conquering power.

"True enough, in ancient China, revolutions placed the peasantry in power or, more precisely, placed the military leaders of peasant uprisings in power. This led each time to a redivision of the land and the establishment of a new 'peasant' dynasty, whereupon history would begin from the beginning; with a new concentration of land, a new aristocracy, a new system of usury, and a new uprising." [16]

Lenin argued that history would decide whether or not the peasantry could assume an independent role in the proposed alliance. Lenin's idea was in effect an 'algebraic formula' as to which class, proletariat or peasantry, would lead the alliance, what the precise complexion of the government would be and how far it would encroach on the powers of the capitalists. Despite all the attempts of Lorimer to defend this formula, its author, Lenin himself, said in April 1917, that history had filled this with a "negative content". He indicated that the task was now for the proletariat to seize power supported by the peasantry. To emphasise this, Lenin also proposed that the Bolsheviks should change their name to the 'Communist Party'.

The Lorimers of that period – Kamenev, Zinoviev and Stalin – opposed Lenin's proposal just as much as they upheld Lenin's old formula of the 'democratic dictatorship'. Trotsky's theory of the permanent revolution was borne out in the October Revolution where the working class assumed power through the soviets and led the multi-millioned peasant masses behind them.

Allied to the discussions within the Russian revolutionary movement over the mutual relations between the working class and the peasantry was the issue of whether or not the peasantry could create its own independent party. The working class, led by the Bolsheviks, came to power, that is established the 'dictatorship of the proletariat' (workers' democracy) and then together with the peasantry carried through the bourgeois-democratic revolution while *at the same time* placing on the agenda socialist, that is 'collectivist', action by the proletariat itself.

A "Leninist Critique"?

But Lorimer disputes all this, counterposing Lenin's 'democratic dictatorship of the proletariat' to Trotsky's ideas of the 'permanent revolution'. In an unbelievable exercise of misquotation, half quotations and innuendo, Lorimer engages in a cynical exercise in historical and political falsification. He throws mud on the ideas that led to the greatest victory of the working class in history. Karl Radek was once a leading member of the Russian Left Opposition but capitulated and made his peace with Stalin by attacking the Theory of the Permanent Revolution. In answering him Trotsky pointed out that Radek *"did not think up a single new argument against the theory of the permanent revolution"*.[17] He was, said Trotsky, an 'epigone' (a slavish, unthinking adherent) of the (Stalinist) epigones of Lenin. Lorimer is the modern Radek, with the qualification that he demonstrates less talent than Radek in his arguments against Trotsky. There is not one new point of criticism in his assault on Trotsky's theory. Without burdening our text with too many abstract points or quotations it is necessary here to briefly outline and answer the criticisms of Lorimer on the permanent revolution. (A fuller answer will have to be made in time but space prevents it in this reply.) Only by doing this is it possible to understand the roots of the DSP's apologia for the Cuban regime. Speaking about the 1905 Russian Revolution Lorimer argues:

"Lenin argued that the completion of the bourgeois-democratic revolution by an alliance of the workers and peasants, led by the Marxist party, would then enable the working class, in alliance with the poor, semi-proletarian majority of the peasantry, to pass uninterruptedly to the socialist revolution." [18]

This is quite wrong. Lenin only occasionally mentions about moving 'uninterruptedly' towards the socialist revolution. This idea, 'uninterrupted' or 'permanent' revolution had been put forward by Trotsky in the book 'Results and Prospects' as we have explained above. Lenin's main idea was that the bourgeois-democratic revolution could have led, could 'stimulate' the socialist revolution in Western Europe, which would then come to the aid of the workers, and peasants in Russia and place 'socialism' on the agenda. If Lenin had consistently advanced the idea outlined by Lorimer then there would have been no fundamental difference between him and Trotsky on the revolution. Indeed the differences between Lenin and Trotsky are indicated a few paragraphs later when Lorimer writes:

"The Bolsheviks believed that the victory of a worker-peasant democratic revolution in Russia would stimulate the proletarian-socialist revolution in the more industrially developed countries of Western Europe. The victory of proletarian-socialist revolutions in Western Europe, in turn, would open the way for the Russian proletariat to advance along the road of the socialist reorganisation of the economy."[19]

Clearly Lenin envisaged a period of development of society and the working class between "the democratic dictatorship of the proletariat and peasantry" coming to power and socialism. There is nothing 'uninterrupted' in this.

Lorimer repeats the legends of the Stalinists that Trotsky underestimated the peasantry, believed that the working class alone could carry thorough the revolution in Russia and was against a real alliance of the peasantry with the working class, etc. There is no better answer to the critics who use this argument than to quote Trotsky himself.

As if answering his latter-day critics like Lorimer, who pore over each and every article of Trotsky to find a difference with Lenin, he writes: *"The devil can quote scripture to his purpose."* In his polemic against Radek he honestly admitted that there were "gaps" in his original Theory of the Permanent Revolution published, it must be understood, in 1906. History, particularly the great experience of the February and October revolutions of 1917 had filled in these "gaps" but in no way had they falsified but rather had reinforced Trotsky's general idea. Look at the honesty with which Trotsky deals with the evolution of his ideas as against the shameful misrepresentation of them by Lorimer. Trotsky writes in his answer to Radek:

"I do not at all want to say that my conception of the revolution follows, in all my writings, one and the same unswerving line…There are articles [of Trotsky] in which the episodic circumstances and even the episodic polemical exaggerations inevitable in struggle protrude into the foreground in violation of the strategic line. Thus, for example, articles can be found in which I express doubts about the future revolutionary role of the peasantry as a whole, as in a state, and in connection with this refused to designate, especially during the imperialist war, the future Russian Revolution as 'national,' for I felt this designation to be ambiguous. But it must not be forgotten here that the historical processes that interest us, including the processes in the peasantry, are far more obvious now that they have been accomplished than they were in those days when they were only developing. Let me also remark that Lenin – who never for a moment lost historical sight of the peasant question in all its gigantic historical

magnitude and from whom we all learnt this – considered it uncertain even after the February revolution whether we should succeed in tearing the peasantry away from the bourgeois and drawing it after the proletariat." [20]

Lorimer makes much of the fact that Trotsky in his earlier writing looked towards an alliance between the working class and the poor peasants rather than the 'peasantry as a whole'. Lenin himself sometimes spoke in the manner that Trotsky did of the proletariat linking up with the poorer layers in the villages, etc. But the key question skirted around by Lorimer was that the working class in the October 1917 revolution led the mass of the peasantry to complete the bourgeois democratic revolution but did not stop there. It then passed in an 'uninterrupted' fashion to begin the socialist tasks in Russia and to spread the revolution internationally. The fantastical schema of Lorimer was that the October revolution was not a socialist revolution but represented the victory of the bourgeois democratic revolution through the 'democratic dictatorship of the proletariat and the peasantry'. This was separated as the 'first stage' (in accordance with the two-stage theory) from the 'socialist revolution', which was only carried through allegedly in the summer and autumn of 1918.

This mechanistic idea, which seeks to artificially separate the completion of the bourgeois democratic revolution from socialist tasks is not only a completely inaccurate assessment of what happened in October 1917 but would be absolutely fatal if applied in the situation existing currently in the neo-colonial world. Lorimer and the DSP, like the Stalinists before them, perceive that the bourgeois-democratic revolution can be carried through by a 'democratic dictatorship of the proletariat and the peasantry'. This is reflected concretely in an alliance between parties and is linked to the idea which Lorimer defends that there can exist "independent" peasant parties which can come together in a coalition government with "workers' parties" to carry through the bourgeois revolution. Contrary to Trotsky's contention in his answer to Radek, that Russian history attests to the fact prior to 1917 that there was no stable independent peasant party, Lorimer points towards the Social Revolutionaries. There were of course peasant formations, or parties purporting to represent the peasantry, in Russia prior to 1917. But all of these existed only in short, relatively stable periods and then flew apart, divided along class lines, in periods of social crisis.

The Social Revolutionaries in 1917 reflected this. After February 1917 they were a prop of the bourgeois coalition together with the Mensheviks and opposed giving land to the peasants. In action, they were repudiated by the majority of the peasants. The Left Social Revolutionaries who split from the SRs, it is true, shared power for a short period after the October revolution. They occupied a minority position compared to the Bolsheviks, which was not clearly envisaged in Lenin's original idea of the democratic dictatorship of the proletariat and peasantry (he left open which class, or which party representing each class, would dominate in the coalition government). Trotsky in his Theory of the Permanent Revolution clearly argued that the working class would dominate and lead the peasantry. Moreover, the rapid separation of the Left SRs from the government itself was a reflection of the growing class conflict at their base, amongst the peasantry as well as an indication of their inchoate middle-class character. Trotsky answered those, like Lorimer today, who argued that the dual power situation between February and October 1917 was a realisation or a partial realisation of the democratic dictatorship when he wrote:

"References to the fact that the democratic dictatorship was 'realised' in the form of the dual power ('in a certain form and up to a certain point') were made by Lenin only in the period between April 1917 and October 1917, that is, **before the actual carrying out of the democratic revolution.**" [21]

It took the coming to power of the working class in October 1917 to carry through the bourgeois democratic revolution and then begin to pass over to the socialist tasks both on a national and an international scale.

Mistaken analysis of the revolution

In all those cases, like in China between 1925 and 1927 and in many other instances in the neo-colonial world where the theory of 'two stages' or of the mangled distorted picture of Lenin's idea of the 'dictatorship of the proletariat and peasantry' have been put into practice, it has resulted in an abortion, the derailment of a revolution or revolutionary situations and the destruction of the flower of the proletariat. It has meant the subordination of the representatives of workers' organisations to petty bourgeois parties, ultimately representing the bourgeois in coalition governments. In other words, the political expression of the outmoded slogan of the 'democratic dictatorship of the proletariat and peasantry' in the modern era has invariably been reflected in popular front or popular front type governments in these countries, which have ended in defeat.

The false position of Lorimer and the DSP on the issue of the permanent revolution has led them to a mistaken analysis on the Cuban Revolution. Their 'two stage theory', they maintain, explains the Cuban Revolution. Fidel Castro first of all carried out a 'democratic' stage, all the time concealing his real 'socialist' and 'communist' views and then some time later proceeds to construct 'socialism'. The reality of the Cuban Revolution is entirely different to this. The momentous events in this revolution in fact, as we hope to show, confirm splendidly Trotsky's Theory of the Permanent Revolution but in a distorted fashion. These distortions, as we shall see, arise in the main because of the absence of a mass revolutionary party in Cuba consciously basing itself on the working class.

Lorimer's criticisms are aimed against a short pamphlet compiled from three separate articles written by myself and first published in 1978. However, his sustained attack on this 20-year old pamphlet has been carried out not in the full light of day, so workers and activists and the world labour movement could learn from the perceived 'errors' of myself, Militant (the present-day Socialist Party) and the CWI. It was published in The Activist, an internal bulletin of the DSP itself! We only learnt of Lorimer's vitriolic attack because we were sent a copy of this bulletin by an Australian sympathiser of ours. The DSP likes to present itself, through its weekly journal Green Left Weekly, as a friendly, approachable 'facilitator' of organisations and left leaders throughout the world, who are genuinely fighting for socialism. Occasionally the mask slips and scathing attacks are unleashed against their opponents in the Australian and world labour movement. The Australian supporters of the CWI, the Socialist Party formerly the Militant Socialist Organisation, have been the recipients of such treatment. Dismissed by the DSP as 'insignificant', the DSP has nevertheless sought to court our Australian organisation, strives to attract them into their ranks and has offered them positions on their national committee while, behind the scenes, secretly and venomously attacking the leadership and the members of the CWI.

This is clearly shown in the language and the methods deployed by Lorimer to 'demolish' our analysis of Cuba. He implies that I have no right to criticise Castro and the Cuban leadership. He writes: *"Taaffe, from the comparative intellectual freedom of 'democratic capitalist' England, is oblivious"* to the great difficulties of the Cuban revolution and state. Militant (the Socialist Party), he argues, has an arid parliamentary schema for Britain. 'Taaffe' also seeks to impose this from 'comfortable' Britain on a poor country like Cuba.

"In his view, the Cuban revolutionists should only have presented a 'clear socialist programme' perhaps like the one he (Taaffe) has presented for nearly a quarter of a century, i.e, with 'socialism' being achieved through the election to parliament of a Labour Party majority armed with an 'enabling act' to nationalise industry!" [22]

We also read about 'Taaffe's' alleged *"fairy tales"* about the Cuban revolution: He dismisses our alleged incurable *"sectarian hostility to Castro"* which is "Castrophobic". To top it all the alleged *"undemocratic regime that Taaffe practises in the CWI"* is thrown in for good measure as proof of the wrong analysis we have made of the Cuban revolution. This all emanates from a leader of a party, the DSP, which bans factions within its organisation and supports a similar position within the Cuban Communist Party (PCC). Contrast this to the methods of the Socialist Party in Britain and the CWI. In the course of disputes over changing our name and in a very intense debate over the formation of the Scottish Socialist Party (SSP) in Scotland, every single written contribution was published in internal material (so much so that the leaders of the DSP complained to me when I visited Australia in 1997 that they could not read all our internal bulletins). Moreover, the Socialist Party has allowed the formation of 'tendencies' and factions unlike the DSP.[23]

Lorimer prefers to concentrate on my pamphlet of 20 years ago, the main lines of which I would still defend, but studiously ignores the current CWI pamphlet by Tony Saunois, 'Che Guevara – Symbol of Struggle', which gives an up-to-date analysis and fills out the sketchy points which I made in 1978.

We will nevertheless seek to reply to Lorimer's attacks on us. We will do this in the order in which he raises them in his article. We have to do this because of the illogical and incoherent way in which he sets out his argument and the presentation of his case. We will not set out the main events of the Cuban Revolution but only touch on them in passing. The interested reader can familiarise themselves with the events by reading our original articles reprinted in this book.

His first main point deals with the character of Cuba following the overthrow of Batista and the liquidation of landlordism and capitalism. Quite erroneous and crude comparisons are drawn with the processes of the Russian Revolution, the character of the state under Lenin and Trotsky, and whether or not Trotsky's Theory of the Permanent Revolution was correct.

Right from the outset we hailed the Cuban Revolution as a colossal step forward. The now deceased leaders of the USFI, chief amongst them Ernest Mandel and Joseph Hansen of the American Socialist Workers Party, also quite correctly greeted the victory of the Cuban revolution. But they gave a quite wrong characterisation of the state that ushered from the revolution. They described the regime of Castro and Che Guevara as the 1960s equivalent of what the Bolsheviks of Lenin and Trotsky established between 1917 and 1923. The latter was a healthy workers' state but with certain 'bureaucratic deformations'. This 'deformation' arose from the isolation of the Russian Revolution, which resulted from the betrayal of the revolutionary wave in Western Europe above all by the leaders of the social democratic organisations. From a Marxist standpoint however, a healthy workers' state with 'bureaucratic deformations' is entirely different to a bureaucratically deformed workers' state.

A healthy workers' state with 'bureaucratic' deformations and a deformed workers' state is the difference between a wart and a monstrous ulcer, an incubus, which threatens to consume the 'body', the planned economy. In the former the task is to 'reform', to correct the bureaucratic deformations through increased workers' control and management, and the spread of the revolution internationally. In a bureaucratically deformed workers' state, a bureaucratic caste has separated itself from the control of the masses.

What is therefore required to establish a healthy workers' state is not 'reform' but the establishment of workers' democracy, which is only possible through a complete change of political regime which in turn requires a political revolution.

The DSP leaders have taken the original analysis of the USFI to its logical conclusion, and are now uncritical cheerleaders of the likes of Castro and any other 'radical' leader or formation, particularly in the neo-colonial world. They believe that Cuba was and still is a healthy workers' state. This is quite clear from what Lorimer writes:

"It is not sufficient to point to instances where the Castro leadership has made mistakes or taken wrong positions on world events. If this were the criteria for deciding that a leadership did not defend the general class interests of the proletariat of its country, then we would have to conclude that such a leadership has never existed anywhere in the world. There has never been a revolutionary proletarian leadership – and this includes Marx and Lenin, not to mention any of their contemporary disciples – who have not made mistakes or taken wrong positions on events occurring in other countries." [24]

Thus Castro is on a par with Lenin and Marx (Trotsky is not included because the DSP has broken with Trotsky's ideas). Lorimer goes on to characterise the Cuban regime as a healthy workers' state:

"A mere listing of bureaucratic deformations in the Cuban political system is not sufficient to substantiate the conclusion that the class interests of the Cuban proletariat can only be defended and advanced through the revolutionary overthrow of the Castro regime. Lenin observed in 1921-22 that the proletarian regime he headed had bureaucratic deformations. But no genuine Marxist would have concluded that this meant that the defence of the class interests of the Russian proletariat at that time necessitated the revolutionary overthrow of the Bolshevik regime.

*As in Soviet Russia, there has been a problem with bureaucratism, of privilege-taking, of corruption of individual officials, in revolutionary Cuba from the start...But they are not the same thing as the **political triumph** of a **crystallised petty-bourgeois social layer** such as was represented in Russia by Stalin".* [25]

We hope to show here that this completely false analysis indicates that the DSP leadership has not understood the Russian Revolution, the state which arose from it or the different forces which shaped the Cuban Revolution and put their stamp on the Cuban state right up to today.

Lenin & Castro

B oth in relation to the class forces involved in the Cuban revolution as well as Castro's political evolution Lorimer and the DSP are guilty of the most crass impressionism. They criticised my pamphlet on Cuba because it is allegedly wrong on Castro's real political position. They dispute our contention that up to 1961 Castro "was no more than a radical, middle-class democrat, whose ideal was democratic capitalist America". The evolution of Castro's thoughts and deeds is not an incidental or secondary question. It illustrates the processes at work in the neo-colonial areas in the period in which the revolution took place. It demonstrates how radical figures in conditions of extreme economic and social crisis can go a lot further than they at first intended. Some of them, as was the case in Cuba, went beyond the framework of capitalism itself.

The crisis in Venezuela has pushed a petty-bourgeois army officer, Chavez, towards an extremely radicalised position. How far he is prepared to go it is not possible to say with certainty in advance. A new world economic crisis will wreak even greater devastation on Latin America and could push Chavez even further towards the left. The movement on the other hand could be halted. Only the absence of a mass revolutionary party with a clear, far-sighted leadership is preventing the elimination of the hated landlord-capitalist regime in Venezuela by a social revolution. Theoretically, it is not excluded that a mass movement could develop along the lines of the Cuban revolution in the neo-colonial world in the next period. On the other hand the absence of the Stalinist states, which acted both as a model for radicalised petty-bourgeois leaders and as an economic reservoir, is an important difference between now and when the Cuban Revolution took place. Nevertheless, the example of Cuba will undoubtedly be invoked in the radicalised and revolutionary waves that impend throughout the world and particularly in the neo-colonial world. It is therefore crucial for the working class to possess a clear understanding of the Cuban Revolution, of its great achievements but also of its limitations – particularly the absence of real workers' democracy – which arose from the way the Cuban Revolution and its main leaders evolved.

On the issue of Castro's political outlook, Lorimer concedes that in an interview with the well-known American journalist Herbert Matthews during the struggle against Batista, Castro had said:

"You can be sure we have no animosity towards the United States and the American people...We are fighting for a democratic Cuba and an end to dictatorship".

But he then goes on to make this criticism of myself:

"Taaffe does not tell us what he expects Castro should have said to a US journalist at that time".[26]

We anticipated the arguments of those like the DSP who argue (in retrospect it might be added) that Castro was pursuing a course of action calculated to throw dust in the eyes of the opponents of a socialist revolution in Cuba. We wrote:

"Perhaps this was a 'crafty ruse' merely meant to fool the landlords and capitalists? On the contrary, all the evidence shows that Castro and his supporters never started off their struggle with a clear socialist programme and perspectives as had Lenin and the Bolsheviks in Russia." [27]

Lorimer disputes this and incredibly tries to recruit Lenin to his position. The Stalinist idea of stages in the revolution in the neo-colonial world is advocated. Lorimer claims that,

"Lenin and the Bolsheviks did not build support among the Russian workers and peasants for the struggle against either the Tsarist autocracy or (after February 1917) the landlord-capitalist Kerensky government, on the basis of a 'socialist programme' (a programme for the wholesale expropriation of bourgeois property in industry)." [28]

This false argumentation fits in with the repudiation by the DSP of Trotsky's theory of the permanent revolution, which correctly anticipated the Russian Revolution and Lenin's April Theses. Lenin, when he arrived at the Finland station in 1917, turned his back on the Social Revolutionary and Menshevik opportunist dignitaries of the Petrograd Soviet and addressed the gathering of workers with the famous phrase: *"I greet you as the advanced guard of the coming world socialist revolution".* A series of transitional demands was put forward by Lenin and the Bolsheviks between February and October 1917, which were absolutely incompatible with the maintenance of landlordism and capitalism in Russia.

Lenin's pamphlet 'The Impending Catastrophe' was in effect a transitional programme proceeding from the day-to-day demands of the Russian workers and peasants, and linking this to the idea of the socialist revolution. In this pamphlet he comes out in favour of taking over, nationalising the 'commanding heights of the economy'. This would have been impossible if, as Lorimer believes, Lenin was not in favour of advocating the socialist revolution before October 1917.

In the April Theses Lenin had come to the same conclusions as Trotsky. He argued that the tasks of the bourgeois democratic revolution could only be completed by the coming to power of the working class allied to the peasantry. The October

Revolution was a socialist revolution. State power was held by the working class, through democratically elected soviets (we will return to this later).

Lorimer argues that Lenin and the Bolsheviks had just as little a worked-out perspective as Castro did in the period prior to 1960. This is because the Bolsheviks did not proceed to nationalise the bulk of industry until compelled to do so by the exigencies of the civil war and the sabotage of the capitalists in the autumn of 1918. Nothing could be further from the truth. The Bolsheviks, prior to coming to power, had envisaged that they would be compelled to take over the 'commanding heights of the economy' in time and said so openly. But in order to give the relatively culturally deprived Russian working class the time to acquire the expertise to control and manage industry, the workers' state left ownership in the hands of the bourgeoisie and a system of workers' control was implemented.

A 40-year debate has taken place over the precise views of Castro prior to his coming to power. One thing is certain however is that he, unlike Lenin, Trotsky and the Bolsheviks, never professed his 'Marxism'. On the contrary Castro went out of his way to distance himself from 'Marxism' and 'Communism'. If, despite all the evidence, Castro was already a 'Marxist' at the time of the revolution (which the DSP claims – and which Castro claimed later) but concealed this for 'tactical' reasons then we believe he was wrong to do so. Could Lorimer give us one example of Lenin between February and October 1917 concealing his views from the workers and peasants of Russia? He clearly agrees that Castro was correct to hide his real views, as we shall see later. This indicates that the DSP has not only gone over to the Stalinist theory of stages in the revolution in the neo-colonial world. They have also borrowed the methods of the Stalinists of seeking to conceal their real programme from the masses for fear of 'frightening them'. However, the evidence of those who participated with Castro in the revolution – rather than those who comment from the 'comfort' of Sydney 40 years later – refute Lorimer's arguments. The same goes for the most informed commentators at the time of the revolution and since.

Carlos Franqui was a heroic participant in the 26 July Movement and in the Cuban Revolution alongside Castro and Che Guevara. In the first period of the revolution he was responsible for 'Castroite propaganda' and was the organiser of the 'Congress of Intellectuals' in Havana at the end of 1967. Given that he was driven into exile by Castro's behaviour his criticisms are naturally sometimes subjective and personal. Nevertheless they come from a 'socialist humanist' standpoint. In his book 'Family portrait with Fidel' he maps out the bureaucratic degeneration of the revolution "almost from its outset". He makes the following comment about Castro's ideological position before the revolution:

*"The questions people were always asking and continued to ask were: Was Fidel a Communist? Had he become a Communist? Is he a Communist? What was his plan? Was it really the Cuban situation – Cuba's economic dependence and the US blockade – that threw Cuba into the clutches of the Soviet Union? No one thought Fidel was a Communist. I mean no one. We knew that Raúl Castro was a Communist, that Che Guevara was also, and that Camilo, Ramiro, Celia, Haydée, and some **comandantes** and other collaborators were Communists, too. But no one knew about Fidel, including me – who saw him at quite close range – and even his most intelligent enemies."* [29]

He also answers Lorimer's assertions that after the Moncada raid and his subsequent trial and imprisonment Castro had become a covert 'Leninist':

"At the trial of the Moncada group, one of Lenin's books appeared among the evidence. It's curious how history changes with time. At the trial, the allegations of Batista's prosecutor about Communist influence were denied. Years later, the same book would be a badge of honour – the first appearance of Lenin in the context of the Cuban revolution. 'History Will Absolve Me' would be Fidel's first political statement, but neither its ideas nor its language reveals a clandestine communism. There is a consistency of thought in all of Fidel's writing and manifestos between 1953 and 1958. He talks about re-establishing the constitution of 1940, about democratic elections, and about reforms. He violently rejects the Batista regime's charges of being a Communist, and, if that were not enough, he forms the 26 July Movement, when the Communists [read Stalinists – PT] were condemning insurrection, guerrilla warfare, and sabotage." [30]

None other than Che Guevara had even written that Castro was a *"left-wing bourgeois"*.[31] Guevara's testimony counts for a little more than Lorimer's historical idealisations. Franqui comments further on Castro's chequered ideological journey:

"In July 1958, out in the Sierra, Fidel made some startling statements to Jules Dubois, an American correspondent with State Department connections. Some of the young radicals from Santiago – Nilsa Espín, Rivero, and the president of the student body, Jorge Ibarra, dropped out of the 26 July Movement because of the conservatism of those remarks. In fact, Fidel's statements were so reactionary they were suspicious. But until the end of the war and the beginning of 1959, no one believed Fidel was a Communist. Now, in 1959, when the agrarian reform had yet to take place and Fidel was more or less incommunicado, Raúl and Che began to take certain matters into their own hands – especially regarding the takeover of plantations by means of Communist peasant leaders. In a public address, Fidel severely criticised those methods, ordered the restitution of the lands, and said that the agrarian reform would be strictly legal. In his visits to the university and to the offices of 'Bohemia' and 'Revolución', he would say in a loud voice: 'I believe only in the revolution. I will shoot

*anyone who opposes the revolution – including Raúl and Che'." * [32]

Franqui once more highlights the empiricism of Fidel Castro, how he responded to and was affected by the situation:

"Fidel wasn't playing some game with Raúl and Che. They didn't know what he was up to. Raúl was so fed up that he said to me one day that if things didn't start changing soon, he was going to fight in Santo Domingo. Again, was Fidel a Communist or not? Let's begin by trying to be objective, which means not taking Fidel seriously when he says, 'I am not now nor have I ever been a Communist. I am and shall forever be a Marxist-Leninist.' Let's begin with Fidel in jail for a year and a half on the Isla de Pinos after the raid on Moncada. He seems to have spent his time reading, carrying out a serious study of Marx, Engels, Lenin, and Trotsky. Lenin fascinated him, but not only Lenin – Robespierre, too." [33]

Castro neither had a 'concealed' nor explicit perspective similar to that of the Bolsheviks nor a programme like Lenin's April Theses up to the seizure of power in Russia in October 1917. This is absolutely clear when we recount the statements of Castro, Che Guevara, and many others who participated in the military guerrilla struggle against the Batista regime. In the proclamation at the time of the attack on the Moncada barracks, and which was to be read after the capture of a radio station in 1953, Castro declared:

"The Revolution declares its firm intention to establish Cuba on a plan of welfare and economic prosperity that ensures the survival of its rich subsoil, its geographical position, diversified agriculture and industrialisation...The Revolution declares its respect for the workers...and... the establishment of total and definitive social justice, based on economic and industrial progress under a well-organised and timed national plan...The Revolution recognises and bases itself on the ideals of Martí and it adopts as its own the revolutionary programme of Joven Cuba, the ABC Radical and the PPC [Orthodoxos]...The Revolution declares its absolute and reverent respect for the Constitution which was given to the people in 1940". [34]

Furthermore, Castro's five measures, which would have been proclaimed had he conquered the Moncada Barracks in 1953, were extremely modest and were in no way incompatible with the continuation of capitalism in Cuba. Hugh Thomas, the noted historian of the Cuban Revolution, comments:

"This programme could not in itself be described as supporting any single political philosophy...It concentrated on the aspects of Cuban society which Castro himself knew – farming and education, housing and social conditions. The plans must have been Castro's own, and it seems likely that he did not consult anyone... Indeed, what seems surprising is the modesty of Castro's approach towards the sugar problem.

*Workers' shares and profits; encouragement of Cuban ownership (already increasing); guaranteed 55 percent **colono** participation in cane production (already normal); movement towards a **colonia** between 150 acres and (say) 1,000 acres – all this was scarcely radical and by itself would not have fulfilled the demand that Cuba should become internationally independent."* [35]

Thomas goes on:

*"Castro made much of the cry of Yara and Baire, of Martí and Maceo: Castro might know something of Marx, might regard those who did not know Lenin as ignoramuses, but he evidently knew Martí much better. Like others before him, he saw himself indeed as Martí, the young man who forced the different groups opposed to Spain into a single movement, the man of heroic phrases as well as deeds, speaker and soldier, enemy of tyrants **par excellence**, incorruptible renewer. Castro embarked on the Moncada attack without indeed a very carefully worked-out ideology, only a desire to overthrow the 'tyrant' Batista and also move on to destroy the whole rotten society, the institutionalised 'normal' violence of old Cuba, of which Batista was a symptom not a cause."* [36]

During the imprisonment that followed the failure of the Moncada attack, as Franqui has pointed out, Castro read Lenin as dozens of other national liberation leaders had done before him and since. This did not mean that by the time that the guerrilla struggle had been launched that he had developed a worked out Marxist ideology with a clear programme and perspective. As mentioned before, in his interview with Herbert Matthews he declared:

"You can be sure that we have no animosity towards the United States and the American people... we are fighting for a democratic Cuba and an end to the dictatorship. We are not anti-military... for we know the men are good and so are many of the officers." [37]

Hugh Thomas goes on to state:

"'Anti-imperialism' and even 'democratic' might of course mean anything. It is clear that Matthews himself saw Castro as a social democrat; but it is not of course certain that this was how Castro saw himself." [38]

Castro himself, ex post facto, after the seizure of power, obviously in an attempt to picture his struggle and those of the guerrillas as more consciously socialist than it actually was, maintained that he'd always been predisposed to a Marxist outlook. And the DSP accepts Castro at his word. The evidence supplied not just by capitalist historians like Hugh Thomas and others, points to the contrary. Guevara himself, an unimpeachable source, declared in October 1960:

"The principal actors of this revolution have no coherent viewpoint."

He went on to add:

"But it cannot be said that they were ignorant of the various concepts of history, society, economics, and revolution being discussed in the world today".[39]

In his book 'Che Guevara', Jon Lee Anderson makes the following comment:

"In general, Che already viewed Fidel's July 26 colleagues [during the guerrilla struggle in the Sierra Maestra] as hopelessly bound by their middle-class upbringings and privileged educations to timid notions of what their struggle should achieve, and he was correct in thinking they held views very divergent from his own. Lacking his Marxist conception of a radical social transformation, most saw themselves as fighting to oust a corrupt dictatorship and to replace it with a conventional Western democracy. Che's initial reaction to the urban leaders reinforced his negative presentiments. 'Through isolated conversations,' he wrote in his diary, 'I discovered the evident anti-communist inclinations of most of them'".[40]

Anderson also comments in relation to Matthews's famous interview with Castro:

"Defining the 'Rebel Army's' political slant in almost the terms of an FDR liberal, Matthews wrote: 'It is a revolutionary movement that calls itself socialistic. It is also nationalistic, which generally in Latin America means anti-Yankee. The programme is vague and couched in generalities, but it amounts to a new deal for Cuba, radical, democratic and therefore anticommunist. The real core of its strength is that it is fighting against the military dictatorship of President Batista...[Castro] has strong ideas of liberty, democracy, social justice, the need to restore the Constitution, to hold elections'."[41]

Castro's Ideology

The views of witnesses, the considered comments of those like Anderson who have carefully weighed the evidence, counts for nothing with Lorimer and the DSP. Castro had 'a cunning plan' that he concealed from the majority of the 26 July fighters, from the peasants also who sustained and helped the guerrillas to victory, and from the mass of the working class of Cuba. If this is so then it shows Castro even before he came to power as a Machiavellian figure. Indeed Franqui details his Bonapartist tendencies, balancing between different groupings within the 26 July Movement, which were to be given free reign after the revolution triumphed. His programme, if the DSP is to be believed, was 'socialism by stealth', which social democratic leaders and the Stalinists have advocated in the past. It is not the same as the genuine ideas of Marxism, of Marx, Engels, Lenin and Trotsky. Che Guevara gave a fitting answer to the 'stealthy' arguments of Lorimer and the DSP. Replying to a member of the 26 July Movement who urged caution in order not to provoke the United States, Che told him:

"So you are one of those who think that we can make a revolution behind the back of the Americans...What a shit-eater you are! We must make the revolution into a struggle to the death against imperialism from the first moment. A true revolution cannot be disguised..." [42]

This contrasts with the earlier statements of Fidel Castro recorded by Tad Szulc on his visit to the USA in 1959. Szulc is a particularly important witness. In writing his book he was given unprecedented access to Fidel Castro. He writes:

"On the issue of communism in Cuba, endlessly raised with [Castro] in Washington, he repeated time after time that 'we are not Communists', that if there happened to be any Communists in his government 'their influence is nothing', and that he did not agree with Communism. To reassure Americans during the post-victory transition period, pending ultimate consolidation, Castro announced that Cuba would not confiscate foreign-owned private property (which meant mainly American-owned concerns), and indeed would seek additional investments to provide new jobs." [43]

Let us assume for a moment that Castro was employing 'adroit tactics' and was really concealing his programme for the socialist revolution. We believe even in this case it would be wrong, as Che Guevara argued, for a Marxist to conceal the fact that we stand for a socialist revolution or a socialist transformation of society. It may be necessary under conditions of struggle against a dictatorship or an autocracy to use skilful language in undemocratic parliaments like the Tsarist Duma, to put forward transitional demands that lead the masses to see the need for a socialist revolution without specifically mentioning socialism. The Bolsheviks, for instance, at one stage, following the defeat of the 1905-07 revolution, were compelled because of censorship to describe themselves as 'Consistent Democrats'. It was also necessary on the eve of the October insurrection to hide from the **ruling class** the precise date and steps in the insurrection that overthrew landlordism and capitalism.

But these were not the conditions faced by Castro or the 26 July Movement, certainly after they had taken power in 1959. It would have been legitimate for Castro to separate himself from the Stalinists, the 'Communists' who played such a baleful role during the Cuban Revolution, but not to use the broad brush of 'We are not Communists'. A conscious, socialist, Marxist leadership would have been aware before and at the time of the revolution of the need to prepare the working class in Cuba and worldwide by explaining the precise character of the revolution and the programme of its leadership. To have proclaimed the need for socialism from the beginning, to accompany this with the programme of workers' democracy – of soviets, election of all officials and the right of recall – would have raised even higher the combativity and consciousness of the Cuban working class. It was only events, the attacks and provocations of US imperialism and the impact of this on the Cuban masses, which pushed Castro hesitatingly and empirically into breaking with landlordism and capitalism.

The leaders of the Cuban Revolution did not have the conscious programme and perspectives of Lenin and the Bolsheviks. However, Lorimer also incredibly pictures Lenin as not advocating socialism after the February Revolution of 1917! It is true that Lenin put forward a series of specific demands, land to the tillers, all power to the Soviets, an immediate peace, workers' control in industry, etc. But the constant theme, the general overall idea that was linked to these demands throughout 1917 was the need for the socialist revolution in Russia as an overture to the world socialist revolution. In the struggle to implement a series of transitional demands the masses would come to understand, including the peasantry, that they could not be realised within the framework of landlordism and capitalism, and therefore would support the idea of a socialist overturn.

This was the essence of Lenin's idea, which despite the arguments of the DSP, coincided with the perspectives of Trotsky in his famous theory of the permanent revolution. It is absolutely incredible to argue, on the basis of one article written in September 1917, that the Bolsheviks did not advocate socialism. This is what Lorimer writes:

"There is not a single reference to 'socialism' or 'socialist revolution' in this whole article." [44]

If the Bolsheviks had not advocated the idea of a socialist revolution then why does John Reed in 'Ten Days that Shook the World', describe Lenin speaking at the meeting of the Second Congress of Soviets following the revolution, using the words: *"We shall now proceed to construct the socialist order"*? [45] Moreover, as John Reed explains, even the peasant soldiers, when challenged by Mensheviks, saw the October revolution as the beginning of the world socialist revolution.

In Lorimer's hands Lenin is transformed from a revolutionary socialist to an insipid, liberal cardboard cutout who never openly explained to the Russian workers and peasants the need for the socialist revolution. He demonstrates thereby a complete ignorance of the real processes of the Russian Revolution. The same goes for his references to Trotsky's 1938 Transitional Programme, which he seeks to use against us. Trotsky opposed tooth and nail the Stalinists' idea of the two stages in the revolution (something consistently advocated today by the DSP). This false idea maintains that movements in the neo-colonial world should be restricted to demands for the completion of the agrarian revolution, the liquidation of feudal heritages, national independence and the overthrow of imperialism, with socialism coming later. Their implementation, Trotsky argued, was organically linked to the idea of the coming to power of the working class in an alliance with the poor peasantry, which would constitute the socialist revolution. The fight for democratic transitional demands was linked to the idea of socialism and the socialist revolution.

Rejecting this approach the DSP advocates that radical and revolutionary movements in the neo-colonial world, as with Cuba in 1959 or in Indonesia today, should avoid proclaiming themselves as 'socialists' or even declare that their ultimate aim is 'socialism'. In the case of Cuba, Lorimer declares:

"If [Castro and the 26 July Movement] **had** *done this then it's highly unlikely that they would have succeeded. That's because in the minds of the overwhelming majority of Cuban workers and peasants, 'socialism' was identified with the Stalinist police-states in Eastern Europe (remember that Castro started his struggle at the height of the Cold War – between Stalin's suppression of the East German workers' uprising in 1953 and Khrushchev's crushing of the 1956 Hungarian workers' revolution)."* [46]

It is worthwhile dwelling on this astonishing idea of Lorimer and the DSP. Capitalism and its ideologists undoubtedly used the existence of the Stalinist regimes as a scarecrow with which to frighten the masses away from genuine democratic socialism, not just in the neo-colonial world but in the indusrialised countries as well. But the way to combat this, for genuine Marxists and socialists, is not to abandon or jettison the programme of socialism. It was and is necessary to separate support for the planned economies of Eastern Europe and the Soviet Union from the horrible caricature of socialism represented by the Stalinist one-party totalitarian regimes.

During the 'Cold War' did the DSP advocate socialism or not? If they did, then they have sinned against one of the commandments laid down by Lorimer in his unfortunate tract; the existence of Stalinist regimes means that Marxists are debarred from advocating a form of democratic, pluralistic socialism. This applies not just to the past, during the 'Cold War', but for the proponents of socialism today. While the one-party totalitarian regimes have largely disappeared, their 'memory lingers on' and undoubtedly their example will be resurrected by bourgeois ideologists once a powerful movement for socialism develops again amongst the working class. The ideology of Fidel Castro, as with most of the 26 July Movement combatants, was heterogeneous. It is undeniable that Castro, while imprisoned, like many other national liberation movement leaders, absorbed some of the ideas of Lenin, Marx, Mao Zedong (certainly this was the case with Guevara), but he did not have an ideology that corresponded to that of Lenin, of Marxism, let alone Trotsky. Nor did he seek to build a movement or party based on the collective experiences of the working class historically. The incapacity of Lorimer to understand the fundamental differences in the social forces involved in the Russian Revolution, as opposed to Cuba, also means that he does not understand the phenomena of the Chinese Revolution of 1944 to 1949, or the development of the Vietnamese revolution, if it comes to that. (Out of the Vietnam protests came the forerunner of what is the DSP today.) In the case of the Russian Revolution the working class led by a conscious Marxist party and leadership played the key role. The revolutionary overthrow of landlordism and capitalism in the neo-colonial world after 1945 largely developed in an entirely different form. It was in the main upon the struggles of the rural masses that the revolution was initially fought.

Lorimer goes to great pains to dispute our contention that the 26 July Movement's struggle was based on the peasantry and the rural population. He does not even pause to consider the fact that the struggle of Castro and Guevara was based on a guerrilla war. Any literate Marxist understands that historically this has not been the traditional method of the working class but of the peasantry. Guevara is quite explicit on this. In 1960 he wrote:

"In underdeveloped Latin America the arena for armed struggle must be basically the countryside."

He rebuked those who

"Dogmatically assert that the struggle of the masses is centred in urban movements, totally forgetting the immense participation of the people from the countryside in the life of all the underdeveloped countries of Latin America." [47]

Guevara in his criticisms of the 'dogmatists' had in mind, of course, the Stalinised communist parties in the Latin American continent who pursued a policy of passivity, advocated a 'two stages' theory, and did not link the struggles of the working class in the cities to the struggles of the rural masses. But both Castro and Guevara, and indeed all the serious writers on the Cuban Revolution understand that the struggle of the 26 July Movement was firstly located in the countryside. Lorimer on the other hand sees Castro's struggle as straddling the rural population and the working class. Trying to fit reality into this arid schema, he disputes the conclusion of all serious accounts of the Cuban Revolution, including those of the leading combatants, that the motive force of the revolution was primarily the rural population.

Nowhere did we say in our pamphlets that Castro based himself 'exclusively' on the peasantry as Lorimer is forced to concede by quoting the statement from our pamphlet: *"Castro and Guevara relied on the peasants and the rural population"*.

Hugh Thomas, when dealing with the class structure of Cuba in the mid-1950s, comments that there were 200,000 families of peasants, of which *"140,000 at least were very poor, owning, renting or 'squatting' on not much more than one **caballeria** of land."* Alongside what he called a *"large peasant population"*, there were in Cuba some 600,000 rural workers, of whom well over half were cane cutters, only employed fully during harvests. He comments:

"Some of these naturally had a few chickens and a little land of their own. Unlike the days of slavery, these workers were clearly differentiated from the 100,000 or so workers on sugar mills, the aristocrats of the labour force, well organised and dominant in the union system, both under the communists (before 1947) and with Mujal (after 1947). Next in social status came the 400,000 families of the Cuban urban proletariat, also well organised in unions".[48]

The guerrilla struggle from late 1956 to the fleeing of Batista in early 1959 was based upon the population in the rural areas. The urban working class was looked towards for material, moral and sometimes industrial support, but the main focus of the struggle, as explicitly described by Castro and Guevara, was in the countryside and based on the rural population. By sleight of hand Lorimer and the DSP argue that because there was a large layer of rural wage workers then it would be wrong to say that the 26 July Movement was based on the 'peasantry and the rural population'. Of course, the existence of a large rural 'proletariat' was important but it did not alter the character of the 26 July Movement being fundamentally based upon the peasantry and the rural population. As the above quote from Hugh Thomas indicates, some of these rural workers, with their chickens and their little piece of land of their own, had a half-peasant, half-working class-consciousness. Their support, moreover, as with the urban proletariat, was an auxiliary to the movement of the guerrillas who were based, we repeat, in the main, on the poor peasantry and the rural population. This put its stamp on the 26 July Movement, which was entirely different to the basis of the Bolshevik Party, which rested upon the conscious movement of the working class in the Russian Revolution.

The arguments of the DSP to the effect that Castro's guerrilla army was based as much on the working class as the peasantry is answered conclusively many times by Guevara:

"The guerrilla fighter is above all an agrarian revolutionary. He interprets the desire of the great peasant masses to be owners of the land, of the means of produc-

tion, of the livestock, of all they have yearned for over the years, of what makes up their lives and also will be their grave".[49]

The DSP drag in by the hair the support of the working class for the guerrillas. Of course there was support for the guerrillas. There was similar support in the Chinese Revolution too but in Cuba and in China what was dominant and what was subordinate in terms of social forces compared to the Russian Revolution was entirely different. The DSP quote but do not answer our contention in which we state:

"Lenin based himself on the working class. He anticipated the workers would lead the poor peasantry in the struggle against Tsarism. Castro and Guevara relied on the peasants and the rural population. The working class only entered the struggle through a general strike in Havana when the guerrillas had already triumphed and Batista was fleeing for his life." [50]

The fact that Castro came to power through a predominantly rural movement shaped the whole character of his movement. It was only the peculiar combination of circumstances that existed which resulted in Castro – who never, to begin with, envisaged going beyond the framework of capitalist democracy – presiding over the expropriation of capitalism in Cuba.

Castro, during the September 1958 offensive

The World Balance of Forces

L orimer, with laboured irony, makes much of our phrase *"peculiar combination of circumstances"* and ridicules the idea that a *"radical middle-class democrat whose ideal was democratic capitalist America"* led a social revolution. For him the political spectrum amounts to simply black and white. Shades of grey, the complex processes that developed in the neo-colonial world in particular, are lost on him. He is therefore incapable not only of understanding the Cuban Revolution, but the earlier Chinese Revolution, the real motive force of the Vietnamese Revolution, events in Angola, Mozambique and elsewhere. These revolutions were 'unique' and had no parallel with previous 'classical' revolutions, above all in Russia. They arose because of the *"peculiar combination of circumstances"* which obtained then.

What were these circumstances? They arose from the relationship of class forces worldwide that emerged after the Second World War. Contrary to what Trotsky expected, Stalinism together with US imperialism emerged strengthened. Because of the political betrayal of the revolutionary wave of 1943 to 1947 in Europe by the communist parties and the social democracy, the political preconditions were laid for the long boom of 1950 to 1973 throughout world capitalism. At the same time, for the majority of countries in Africa, Asia and Latin America the bourgeois democratic revolution remained incomplete. Also, as we have seen, Trotsky's theory of the Permanent Revolution holds that the only class capable of rallying the majority of the 'nation' – the poor peasant masses and the urban petty bourgeois – is the organised working class. Having carried through the bourgeois democratic revolution it would then use the power that it wields to go over to the socialist tasks of the revolution within a national framework but also internationally as well.

If the Russian Revolution is viewed as a purely national event then the Mensheviks were correct against Lenin, Trotsky, the Bolsheviks and Rosa Luxemburg. Russia, a predominantly agrarian industrially backward country, with 80 per cent of the population in the countryside, was not ready for socialism. Marx himself had pointed out that the beginning of socialism would necessitate a higher level of technique and productivity of labour than that reached by the highest capitalist country in the world, which today is capitalist America. Russia was much removed from this position. But, in the words of Lenin, Russia was the 'weakest link in the chain of world capitalism' which by taking to the road of revolution could also be the spark for a world revolution.

Lenin had this perception, even when his programme was for a 'democratic dictatorship of the proletariat and peasantry' (which he subsequently abandoned in favour of the 'dictatorship of the proletariat', that is a democratic workers' state or a workers and peasants' government). Lenin's idea was that an alliance of the working class and the peasantry could begin the process of completing the bourgeois revolution in Russia. This in turn would provoke the socialist revolution in the West, in Germany for instance, which would then feed back into Russia itself where the socialist tasks would be posed. There is nothing of Lenin's internationalism, of seeing revolution in one country as a link in a process of world revolution, and of understanding that only the working class is capable of developing a consistently internationalist outlook, in the writings of Lorimer and the DSP. The essence of the situation at the time of the Cuban revolution is that these classical conditions for permanent revolution, which were realised in the Russian Revolution, could not develop in the same way in the neo-colonial world in the post-1945 period.

On the one side there was, and is, the complete bankruptcy of landlordism and capitalism in the neo-colonial world. This was the case even during the economic upswing of 1950-1973 when some of the countries in the neo-colonial world benefited from the few crumbs which fell from the table of the industrialised countries. The national bourgeoisie in these countries were weak and incapable of taking society forward. The 'Tigers' in South East Asia were an exception. Ironically it was the US – in Japan – or the US client regime in Taiwan, which carried through from above one of the main tasks of the bourgeois democratic revolution, the expropriation of the landlords. This was necessary because of the challenge posed by the newly victorious Stalinist regime in China. This was a key factor, together with access to the US market, in clearing the way for the development of capitalism and the spectacular growth rates that the Tigers enjoyed up to the 1990s. The working class, on the other hand, because of the false policies of the leaders of the mass communist parties in many countries under the sway of Stalinism and reformist leaders, were blocked from playing the role that the Russian working class played in October 1917. The impasse in society, at the same time, affected the middle layers in society including the petty bourgeois officer caste who felt keenly the backwardness of their societies, their incapacity to go forward on the basis of outmoded landlordism and capitalism, and looked for a way out.

Some of these radicalised petty bourgeois elements came from a Stalinist or ex-Stalinist background. Thus Mao Zedong and Zhou Enlai, following the defeat of the

1925-27 Chinese Revolution, retreated to the countryside and formed the Red Army. This army was largely based upon the peasantry, which in turn shaped the outlook of its leaders, in the words of Trotsky "the ex-leaders" of a workers' party. The embryo of a new state and with it a bureaucracy existed in the areas under the control of the Red Army during the second world war. The end of that war, with the complete discrediting of the landlord-capitalist regime of the Kuo Min Tang under Chiang Kai Shek opened up a huge vacuum in Chinese society. When the Red Army entered the cities the outline of a bureaucracy already existed, which was hostile to the organised working class and the idea of workers' democracy. However, there was no way forward on the basis of the old society. Therefore Mao and the Red Army balancing between different sections of society, the peasantry, the working class and sections of the bourgeois gradually expropriated landlordism and capitalism, carried through the nationalisation of land and most of industry, and thereby established right from the outset a bureaucratically deformed workers' state. This bore out the main lines of Trotsky's theory of the permanent revolution, although in a caricatured form. Of course, the conscious role of the working class as the leader of the revolution was a vital ingredient of Trotsky's theory. This was absent in China and in Cuba. Therefore, in a certain sense, there is here a partial negation of Trotsky's theory of the Permanent Revolution. A social revolution, the elimination of landlordism and capitalism, takes place but without the working class playing a directly leading role. Nevertheless, because of the peculiar balance of forces nationally and internationally, above all because of the complete blind alley for these societies on the basis of capitalism, a Bonapartist elite resting on a peasant army balances between the classes and presides over a social revolution. However, what emerges is a deformed workers' state rather than a state in which the working class and poor peasantry exercise direct control and management of industry and society through democratically elected soviets or councils.

Khrushchev and the Cuban Revolution

In the schema defended by Lorimer such a development is impossible. How did the Chinese Stalinist regime, a planned nationalised economy but with a one-party totalitarian regime, come into existence other than by the 'peculiar balance of forces' that arose from the second world war, which were not completely foreseen by Trotsky? Moreover, what does Lorimer and the DSP have to say about events in Eastern Europe where a similar process developed, this time through the agency of Russian Stalinism, which presided over the expropriation of the factories and the land from the indigenous capitalists and landlords who had fled? Trotsky said: "Against a lion you use a gun, against a flea you use your forefinger and thumb." This was all that was required in Eastern Europe in order to snuff out the last vestiges of capitalism and landlordism. This led to the establishment of societies and states in the image of Moscow, that is, planned economies with Stalinist political regimes. Right from the beginning there was not the slightest element of workers' control or management which would have been a mortal threat to the political monopoly of the Stalinists.

The Cuban Revolution both in the character of its leading figures and in the way in which it unfolded did differ from what happened in China or Eastern Europe. Castro, Guevara and the other leaders of the 26 July Movement came from outside of the Stalinist tradition, were initially open and showed exemplary revolutionary courage and daring in the military and political struggle against the Batista regime and afterwards. There were also other important differences, which we will come to later on, with what happened in Eastern Europe and China. But, nevertheless, the same general fundamental conditions existed: the bankruptcy of Cuban landlordism and capitalism, the relative political paralysis of the working class due to the perfidious role of the leadership of the Partido Socialista Popular (PSP), Cuba's pre-revolution Communist party, the massive discontent of an increasingly radicalised middle layer, from which Castro came, and the blunders of the Eisenhower administration in the USA.

Lorimer derides the idea that the 'mistakes' of US imperialism helped to radicalise Castro and Cuba and forced them into a break with landlordism and capitalism. However, observers, by no means sympathetic to Castro, on the scene at the time bear out our original analysis that Nixon and Eisenhower were crude in their handling of Castro and Cuba and made a number of 'mistakes'. Philip W Bonsal, the US ambassador in Havana at the time, wrote afterwards that in the spring of 1959:

"Castro's scenario at this time did not contemplate the massive help in the form of economic aid and weapons that he later received from the Soviet Union…[he] became oriented towards dependence on the Soviet Union only when the United States, by its actions in the spring and summer of 1960, gave the Russians no choice other than to come to Castro's rescue."

Tad Szulc also underlines Bonsal's impressions:

"It is certainly arguable that if the United States had not threatened his survival Castro might have chosen domestic Marxist solutions without becoming wholly dependent on the Russians economically and militarily – Yugoslavia and China are not such far-fetched analogies. Moreover, at least a year elapsed before Soviet assistance began arriving on the island, and before that Washington need not have closed off all the alternatives." [51]

How far Castro would have moved towards 'domestic Marxist solutions' and whether this would have resulted in a break with landlordism and capitalism is open to debate. What is indisputable is that the crude, threatening blunders of the US administration at the time speeded up the process of the elimination of capitalism and drove Castro into the arms of Moscow. The Russia Stalinists for their part had no prior knowledge of the main figures in the Cuban Revolution, or of where the Cuban Revolution was going. Like most other observers their conclusion, correct as it happens, despite what Lorimer says, was that the leaders of the 26 July Movement were pretty typical of Latin American revolutionaries in the past. Alexander Alexiev, a KGB agent, who was instructed to make contact with Castro and Guevara, wrote that he was originally

"Suspicious about Fidel's true political inclinations and, as he admitted later, had not given Cuba his full attention. 'I didn't think much about the Cuban revolution. I thought it would be like any other (bourgeois) Latin American revolution...and I wasn't sure it was a very serious thing'. " [52]

Giorgi Kornienko, another 'high-ranking Soviet official', wrote about the Kremlin's attitude following Castro's victory:

"I remember in January 1959 when Castro proclaimed a new regime Khrushchev asked the department: 'What kind of guys are these? Who are they?' But nobody knew how to answer his question... not the Intelligence Services, not the Foreign Relations Ministry, not the International Department of the Central Committee. In reality, we didn't know who these guys in Havana were. We sent a telegram to our office abroad, later to Intelligence and others. A few days later, we received a telegram from one of the Latin American capitals – I think Mexico – with some information about Castro and his people. And there was information to the effect that, if not Fidel himself, maybe Raúl... very possibly Che... and some other people close to Fidel had Marxist points of view. I was present when this information was given to Khrushchev. 'If it's really like this,' he said, 'if these Cubans are Marxist and if they develop some sort of socialist movement there in Cuba, it would be fantastic! It would be the first place in the Western Hemisphere with a socialist or pro-socialist government. That would be very good, very good for the socialist cause!'" [53]

Anderson goes on to comment:

"There was certainly lingering scepticism about Castro's revolution in the Kremlin, for what had happened in Cuba was not in the Soviet playbook... The party was not in control, Fidel Castro was still an unknown quality. Even if signs were promising – Fidel had allowed the party to play a role and the men closest to him (Che and his brother Raúl) were Marxists - the jury was still out". [54]

Khrushchev, a shrewd representative of Russian Stalinism, understood what happened. Szulc again comments:

"Khrushchev said that the United States was trying to drive Castro to the wall instead of establishing normal relations with him, adding: 'That's stupid, and it's the result of the howls of zealous anti-communists in the United States who see red everywhere, when possibly some things are only rose-coloured or even white... Castro will have to gravitate to us like an iron filing to a magnet'." [55]

There was a yearning in Cuba for the overthrow of the Batista regime and for solutions to the accumulated problems of an incomplete capitalist democratic revolution.

Castro's Evolution

The struggle of the guerrillas, initially actively supported by the peasant and rural masses, and passively so by the working class, managed to defeat the Batista regime because of the growing hostility of the mass of the population to what this regime represented and the blind alley into which Cuban society had landed. There are many examples in history of individual leaders, with equal daring, tenacity and flair as Castro and Guevara. Both Mao and Tito led genuine mass struggles, demonstrated considerable initiative, in the struggle against the old regime. In this sense they were different to Stalin, a mediocre character, who played no independent role but was rather a grey figure in the Russian Revolution. The same could not be said for Mao or Tito. Nevertheless their regimes, despite the independent evolution of their leaders, and the national antagonisms and clashes with Stalinist Russia were basically states similar to what existed in Russia. Despite their national hostility to Stalin, they started where Stalin finished in 1937, with the construction of Stalinist regimes in China and Yugoslavia.

The precise way that the revolution developed in Cuba took a somewhat different form. Lorimer and the DSP argue that the views of Castro and Guevara evolved in the course of the struggle before the revolution. Yes, they did evolve but they did not have a conscious programme and plan to carry through the socialist revolution. Lorimer uses quotes from the works of Maurice Zeitlin on the issue of 'privileges', which we will comment on later. Yet the same author in his book 'Cuba – an American Tragedy' shows Castro's limits in one of his interviews in 1958:

"Let me say for the record that we have no plans for the expropriation or national-isation of foreign investments. True, the extension of government ownership to certain public utilities – some of them, such as the power companies, US-owned – was a point of our earliest programmes; but we have currently suspended all planning on this

matter. I personally have come to feel that nationalisation is, at best, a cumbersome instrument. It does not seem to make the State any stronger, yet it enfeebles private enterprise. Even more important, any attempt at wholesale nationalisation would obviously hamper the principal point of our economic platform – industrialisation at the fastest possible rate. For this purpose, foreign investment will always be welcome and secure here." [56]

The hesitation, the lack of conscious foresight and the confusion as to where precisely they were heading was evident in the statements of even the boldest of the leaders of the revolution in the first period. Thus in a discussion with Jean-Paul Sartre in 1960 Che Guevara declared:

"They ask us for ideas, a doctrine, forecasts. But they forget that we are a rebound revolution." [57]

In an interview with Laura Berquist from 'Look' magazine in November 1960 he explained:

"What lies ahead depends greatly on the United States. With the exception of the agrarian reform, which the people of Cuba desired and initiated themselves, all of our radical measures have been a direct response to direct aggressions to powerful monopolists of which your country is chief exponent. US pressure on Cuba has made necessary the 'radicalisation' of the revolution. To know how much further Cuba will go, it will be easier to ask the US government how far it plans to go." [58]

Castro, Lorimer argues, on the basis of the evidence of his prison diary and having read Lenin, had become a conscious Marxist who all along was secretly preparing for the socialist revolution. Yet, as we have pointed out, very authoritative witnesses and commentators contradict the thesis of the DSP. Jon Lee Anderson reports a conversation between Che Guevara and David Mitrani (a friend and colleague of Guevara's in Mexico prior to the 1956 Granma landing). He comments:

"Eventually, Che spoke candidly with Mitrani about the revolution, telling him: 'By the first days of August, we're going to transform this country into a socialist state.' At least that was what he hoped and expected, Che said, explaining that Fidel himself was not yet totally convinced because he wasn't himself a socialist; Che was still trying to convince him." [59]

This was not **before** the revolution but in 1960 **after** the expropriation of domestic and foreign capital had begun. Guevara was clearly a heroic figure with socialist and communist inclinations but was without a clear Marxist perspective and programme. The same could not be said of Castro. He was pushed and shaped by his experiences in the war against Batista, by the enormously aroused expectations of the masses in the revolution and, yes, by the 'mistakes' of US imperialism in its threats, blackmail and eventual armed counter-revolutionary invasion in the 'Bay of Pigs', in order to overthrow the Castro regime.

The prevarication and the hesitation of Castro as to which road he would take is testified by those who closely collaborated with him soon after the overthrow of Batista. For instance, one of the Cuban delegates attending an Inter-American conference in Argentina in 1959 said of Castro's views then:

"My impression then was that he was contemplating the possibility of staying on the American side of the fence... as the leader of a Nasser-type revolution in Cuba and Latin America".

However, this source quite correctly comments:

"I do not think the United States would have been willing to pay the price at that moment... As a matter of fact, the Cuban people still don't know the type of social revolution, if any, with which Washington would be willing to negotiate." [60]

In fact Washington believed that by a combination of pressure, support for military incursions, threats of an economic blockade and backed up by the threat of invasion Castro could be brought to heel. Such methods had worked previously, for instance in the case of Guatemala, and the Eisenhower-Nixon White House believed that they would be successful in Cuba. But they only succeeded in pushing Castro into a more and more radical stance, whipping up mass opposition amongst the Cuban population as a whole to US imperialism and compelling Castro to look for alternative means of military and financial support. This he found in the Russian Stalinist regime of Khrushchev. We have described in our pamphlet how the events leading to a break with capitalism unfolded so we will not repeat them here.

Once US capitalism embarked on the steps towards an embargo Khrushchev, representing Russian Stalinism, stepped in. They supplied the market for Cuban sugar and provided the oil that kept the Cuban economy afloat, as well as some of the arms for use against an expected US-financed invasion. The masses acquired arms and were encouraged to do so by Castro and his regime. Lorimer states that this action is conclusive proof of democratic involvement of the masses and the genuine socialist and Marxist consciousness of Castro. He also contends that these are indications that Cuba was a relatively healthy workers' state, as does the fact that Castro initiated and encouraged on 28 September 1960 the formation of the Committees to Defend the Revolution (CDRs). These committees were to be a

"Network of civic organisations, with the inhabitants of each block in every town and city of Cuba forming a committee to ensure the implementation of revolutionary

*decrees and to provide a grassroots vigilante network for the State Security appara-
tus".* [61]

But this was not the first time in history that the masses or a section of them at
least, had been armed to eliminate landlordism and capitalism by forces that were
anything but consciously socialist or democratic. The Stalinists in Czechoslovakia in
1948 created 'militias', called a general strike and based themselves, formally at
least, on the working class. This was enough to eliminate the weak remains of
capitalism in Czechoslovakia. However, no sooner had this been completed than the
masses were disarmed. Subsequently any independent individual let alone a
conscious Marxist or revolutionary was arrested or liquidated by the Stalinists
Czechoslovakia.

The process did not develop like this in Cuba. The Castro government felt its way
forward in a situation of extreme social and political flux and undoubtedly had a
much greater mass popular base than did the 'Communist' parties in Eastern
Europe in the late 1940s. Nevertheless there was no conscious control or management of the state and society. For instance, on May Day 1960 Castro spoke to a Plaza
de la Revolución packed with armed Cubans marching past his podium. According
to Jon Lee Anderson he praised the new militias, warned of an impending US
invasion but
*"He also took the opportunity to make two important points clear: If **he** died Raúl
[Castro's brother] would take his place as prime minister. What's more, there were not
going to be any elections; since the 'people' ruled Cuba already, there was no need to
cast votes. The crowd cheered, repeating the catchphrase 'Revolución Sí, Elecciones
No!' and a new slogan: 'Cuba Sí! Yanqui No!'"* [62]

In the circumstances of 1960 it was correct for Castro and his government to act
quickly against native and foreign capital. But in this episode there is a striking
illustration of the lack of conscious collective control and management by the
masses through their own democratic organisations. It also indicates the plebiscitary character of the government. Plebiscites are the usual methods of Bonapartist
regimes. The masses are there to shout 'Yes!' or 'No!' but not to debate, to discuss
and above all to decide on the measures proposed by the government, nor to elect
and control officials at every level of the state.

Carlos Franqui makes the following illuminating comment about the formation
of the militias:
*"On May Day, 1959, the militia paraded through all the streets of Cuba. A new
instrument of the revolution made its debut: the blue shirts and trousers of the militia,*

whose uniform – once that of common labourers – became the symbol of the new revolutionaries. They were volunteers, they were hard workers, and they were somewhere between soldiers and civilians. They represented spontaneity and organisation. The militiaman was the third hero of 1959. He was the collective hero, the true 'Party of the Revolution.' Men, women, young, old, black, mulatto, workers, peasants, students, professional people, intellectuals, middle-class people, the poor. The militia was the new revolution that gave an identity to all, without prejudice. It asked only for volunteers; it gave military training, it provided care for factories, and it endowed all with political and human awareness. It was armed democracy and came to have a million members.

"Who created it? It was in the air, but it was the unions and the 26 July Movement that provided the impetus. But it was rapidly taken over by those who were in just the right place to do so: the army, with Raúl and the Communists[63] right behind it. But there were conflicts from the outset, because the militia represented egalitarian freedom, and the army demanded obedience to higher authority. An armed people are not an army. And this populist spirit showed just what it could do in the sugar-cane campaigns, in the literacy campaign, and in the fighting that took place in the Escambray Mountains against the anti-Castro rebels. The militia never had the repressive character of the Security Police or the Defense Committees, and the army. The militia was an instrument of revolutionary democracy, the libertarian phase of the Cuban Revolution.

"The militia was used, but no one [in the government] had any confidence in it. That would have required those in power to share power with a revolutionary institution at the popular level. This would be the second time the Cuban Revolution would lose an opportunity to have a people's organisation. First the 26 July Movement was discarded, later it would be the militia. The Russo-Castroite concept that began to take shape and control created an elitist power structure: the people were organised into cadres, watched over and administered by Security, the army, and the bureaucracy. There was only one chief who held all the power." [64]

Role of Stalinism and "Trotskyists"

It does not even occur to Lorimer to ask why the Khrushchev *Stalinist* regime was prepared to extend both political and material support to the Castro regime, while in the case of the Hungarian Revolution of 1956 there was no compromise. The Stalinists then had no alternative from their standpoint but to drown that political revolution, the Hungarian Commune, in blood.

Moreover, in Spain between 1936 and 1938 the Stalinists acted as the most counter-revolutionary force in suppressing and annihilating the Spanish Revolution.

Trotsky explained that the hot flames of the Spanish Revolution with the conscious organisation and mobilisation of the working class terrified the Russian Stalinist regime. This was one of the factors, which led to Stalin's purge trials, which represented a one-sided civil war against the remnants of the Bolshevik party. It was a pre-emptive strike by Stalin and the bureaucracy to prevent a political revolution in Russia that would have followed a successful socialist revolution in Spain.

If the Castro regime had been a healthy or relatively healthy workers' state, with mild bureaucratic 'deformations', as the DSP argue, why is it that Khrushchev and the Stalinist regime in Russia could come to terms with it? They did not see Castro and even Guevara, their government and state, in the process of formation, as constituting a huge threat. It is quite clear from all the accounts from the time that they perceived the establishment of a 'socialist' Cuba in the 'jaws of US imperialism' as adding considerably to their power and prestige. There were later clashes between Castro and the representatives of Russian Stalinism. But at bottom this was a clash between the different national bureaucratic regimes they rested on: one, which was consolidated in Russia, the other in the process of formation. A socialist Cuba based upon workers' and peasants' councils, with the right of recall of all officials, clear limitations on differentials and power clearly vested in the working class and its allies would have constituted a colossal danger to the Stalinist bureaucracy. In this situation there would have been no possibility of a compromise.

And there was the possibility of establishing such a democratic regime in Cuba at the beginning. Che Guevara was searching for an answer to the increased bureaucratism but finally left Cuba after his struggle had failed. The tragedy was that there was no genuine Trotskyist organisation in Cuba which could have helped those Cuban revolutionaries, like Guevara, to discover the real ideas of Leon Trotsky and particularly his analysis and programme for combating bureaucratism in a workers' state. The main Trotskyist organisation, the Trotskyist Revolutionary Workers Party (Posadist) was completely ultra-left in their approach towards the Cuban Revolution and the Cuban government. They were the other side – ultra-leftism – of the coin to the DSP's opportunist adaptation towards the Cuban Revolution and its main figures.

Che Guevara was vaguely aware of Trotskyism. He had read some of Trotsky's works. Yet, in an interview with Maurice Zeitlin he shows his hostility to the Cuban 'Trotskyists' because of their approach. Zeitlin asks Guevara:

"What about the Trotskyists, for example? Carleton Beals pointed out recently that their press here has been smashed and they were unable to complete printing copies of Trotsky's 'The Permanent Revolution'."

The Partido Socialista Popular, the Cuban Stalinist party, had attacked and smashed the presses that printed the Trotskyist journal 'Voz Proletaria' in April 1961. Only a mimeographed publication was published after this. Guevara's response was:

"That did happen. It was an error. It was an error committed by a functionary of second rank. They smashed the plates. It should not have been done. However, we consider the Trotskyist party to be acting against the revolution. For example, they were taking the line that the Revolutionary Government is petty bourgeois, and were calling on the proletariat to exert pressure on the government and even to carry out another revolution in which the proletariat would come to power. This was prejudicing the discipline necessary at this stage."

When asked about Trotskyists in general Guevara replied:

"Here in Cuba – let me give an example. They have one of their principle centres in the town of Guantánamo near the US base. And they agitated there for the Cuban people to march on the base – something that cannot be permitted. Something else. Some time ago when we had just created the workers' technical committees the Trotskyists characterised them as a crumb given to the workers because the workers were calling for the direction of the factories."

In answer to other questions Guevara stated:

"What is to be condemned is that after free discussion and a majority decision, a defeated minority works outside of and against the party – as Trotsky did, for example. To do so is counter-revolutionary." [65]

Che Guevara was entirely wrong in this criticism of Trotsky, who went to great lengths in the beginning to remain within the Russian Communist Party; but was expelled because he symbolised the workers' opposition to the rise and crystallisation of the bureaucracy. This exchange illustrates a number of things. On the one side the completely ultra-left position of the Cuban 'Trotskyists' who were calling for the overthrow of Castro and Guevara while these two enjoyed the mass support of the workers and peasants of Cuba. At no time did we advocate such a crude position as this, as Lorimer implies in his attack on us. We adopted a friendly positive attitude to the revolution and its leading figures. We advocated for Cuba in 1959 and the early 1960s the establishment of workers' and peasants' committees and the programme of workers' democracy. A genuine Marxist approach was to positively support all the progressive measures of Castro and Guevara and the leaders of the revolution, while offering friendly suggestions as to how to create a workers' democracy to ensure the gains and advance the revolution. To propose a march on the Guantánamo base, which Guevara claimed was the proposal of the Cuban 'Trotskyists', would easily be perceived as a provocation and give US imperialism the excuse to intervene against the revolution. The limitations in Guevara's own ideology at this stage and the negative impression made on him by the Cuban 'Trotskyists' were factors in him being unable to work out a rounded-out analysis of the process of bureaucratisation that was taking place in Cuba and which he instinctively opposed. His consciousness of the growing bureaucratisation of the revolution was undoubtedly a major factor in his decision to leave Cuba in 1965.

Workers' Democracy — Did it Exist?

Carlos Franqui wrote about the possibilities at the beginning and his disappointment at the growth in power of the elite:

"The fact of the matter is that we had the possibility of establishing our own Cuban socialism because the working class, the peasants, the youth of the nation, and a goodly sector of the middle classes were with us. The nation was coming into its own because it had taken back its wealth, had recovered its dignity, and was both free and independent.

"This was the moment to have confidence in the people and to create new ways of life. To socialise our major industries would have been easy. The sugar workers were already politicised, and it would have been relatively simple to show them that they could work just as hard for their own interests as they had worked for the boss. The same applied to the cattle industry, which was in fact already supplying the nation with cheap milk and meat. Other industries, like tobacco, would also fall into line. We could stimulate the fishing industry and stop importing cooking oils – an absurdity in a country producing peanuts, corn, and sunflowers. We could turn to the people, to their long experience with the land. And land reform itself would be no problem because only a small minority of the peasants were freeholders, and most of these because the revolution gave them land. We possessed a sound transportation system, so distribution was no problem. Even the professional classes – including ten thousand physicians – supported the revolution. The counter-revolutionary bourgeoisie was already in the United States; good riddance to them. There was no real opposition to the revolution anywhere in Cuba. (Abroad, of course, opposition existed, but it could not, without US assistance, topple the revolution.)" [66]

Franqui goes on to show the raging debates and discussions which took place between the leaders of the revolution on which direction to take, towards greater control and management by the working class and poor peasantry, or towards the Russian 'soviet model'. Like Che Guevara, Franqui was by no means clear as to what needed to be done but his comments show that there was opposition to the increased reliance on Stalinist Russia and the inevitable bureaucratisation that went with it.

"All we needed was to give power to the people – not to a military dictator. We did not need the Russian model, or any Soviet influence. Our thesis, as Comandante Daniel put it in his polemic with Che Guevara, was, 'We want to be free of Yankee imperialism, but we don't want to run into Russian imperialism[67] in getting away from the United States.' ...Russian spare parts were useless for US-made machines. Russia didn't make the things we needed. And its economy, state-run instead of socialist, had already shown in Eastern Europe and China just how inefficient the Russians were. Besides, great powers like to control small ones.

"In conversations with Fidel, we expressed our concerns about the Soviet Union and the models it offered, particularly its tendency to state monopoly instead of real socialism. Some of Fidel's decisions bothered us: state-owned farms instead of self-regulating co-operative farms. A tendency to gigantism: where there had been one huge plantation, Fidel combined ten and made a superplantation. We wanted small-scale agriculture so that we would not be substituting for the old boss a new administrator, for the old owner a new, state owner. But Fidel had an innate distrust of the people; he preferred militarisation to organisation. He also thought that in peacetime and in economics the same rules applied as in wartime and guerrilla fighting – that a group of leaders could change everything. It just wasn't so." [68]

He goes on to point out that it was Fidel Castro's strategy to involve

"The Soviet Union by rapidly deploying the structures of the Soviet state – the Communist Party and a State Security agency. But even the Soviet government was unwilling to comply. The Soviets advised patience and constantly warned us, before and after the fact, about turning Cuba into a socialist state. All Soviet emissaries, ambassadors – even Khrushchev and Mikoyan – recommended calm and patience. As did China and the Eastern bloc nations. They were all shocked at the accelerated and artificial process of nationalisation they saw us engaged in. The more they worried, the faster Fidel went. He envisioned a new kind of government – a Russian structure, but with himself at the top – that would be perfect for Third World nations. In that social structure, the role of the people was to work and to obey unquestioningly.

*"Fidel thought those of us who had taken part in the revolution were not really ready for socialism. This was not true: we were not ready to accept Russian non-socialism, not ready to accept a new **caudillo**. In a discussion with me, Fidel said that the only people in Cuba who knew anything about socialism were the old Communists and that I ought to set aside my prejudices against them and the Soviet Union. He believed, as he said, that the people were not yet ready for socialism, and that Stalinism had been the only way the revolutionary minority in the Soviet Union had been able to impose the revolution on a non-revolutionary majority. I must point out that, at that particular moment, there existed no political apparatus in Cuba. Fidel had caused the 26 July Movement to vanish and had liquidated the Directorio in his two*

speeches of January 1959. The free trade unions, the popular militia, the revolution-ary press, and their adherents were struggling against the reactionaries, the old Communists, and Soviet influence. Raúl, Ramiro, Che, and even Fidel himself had begun to attack us. The government had begun its war against the people. The people resisted, but Fidel possesses the power that turned them from protagonists into obedient servants." [69]

The very simple axiom: 'He who pays the piper calls the tune' applies in the reciprocal relations between Castro's Cuba and the Russian Stalinist regime. Khrushchev was prepared to give aid, as a means of enhancing the position of Russian Stalinism. This was not done in order to further revolution throughout the world, certainly not to sustain a 'healthy workers' state'. Indeed, as Franqui hints, the Stalinist bureaucracy did not necessarily wish to see the establishment of even a deformed workers' state in Cuba. They did nothing to encourage Castro in the course of the struggle, and indeed as the example of Nicaragua in the 1980s demonstrated, if given the choice would actively discourage states in the neo-colonial world from breaking with landlordism and capitalism. Their prime purpose was to specifically enhance the position of Russian Stalinism particularly in its relations with US imperialism. (The DSP are wide of the mark when they criticise us for using the term 'Russian' in relation to the USSR. All the states in the 'USSR' were, in effect dominated by the centralised Russian bureaucracy.) Therefore, while not necessarily encouraging the formation of a deformed workers' state once faced with the accomplished fact Khrushchev and Russian Stalinism were quite prepared to come to its aid. This was for many reasons, not least of which was the fact that such a regime would be an enormous irritant to US imperialism in its own 'backyard'.

The DSP and Lorimer make a lot of the fact that Castro ratified the formation of the militia and that the privileges of the state and army officers were very limited. He draws a favourable comparison between Cuba and China in 1956. He argues, quite falsely, that the differences between the living standards of the Chinese workers and peasants and those of the top echelons of the Chinese bureaucracy were vastly greater than those between the top echelons of the Soviet bureaucracy and the Russian workers in the 1960s and 1970s. Quite apart from crude statistics, in real terms the differences were much greater if one takes into account the many 'hidden' privileges of the bureaucracy in the USSR. In China in the first period after Mao's victory, given the low economic and cultural level of society, there could not be huge differentials. Even in the first period of the Stalinist degeneration in Russia, on paper the privileges of the growing bureaucratic elite were not huge. In fact, the memory of the revolution, with its ideals of equality, was still fresh in the minds of the masses. It would take further isolations of the Russian Revolution, as a result of the defeat of revolutions internationally, which in turn resulted from the false policies of Stalin and his entourage, for the ground to be prepared for the complete abolition of the egalitarian principles of the revolution and a huge widening of differentials.

In Cuba in the first period the differentials were very small, and in the case of Castro and Guevara (certainly the latter) if anything they accepted less than the average Cuban wage at that stage. But, given the limited forces which constituted the 26 July Movement, Castro and Guevara were compelled to draw into important positions in the state machine the heavily bureaucratised PSP, as well as utilising those elements from the old bureaucracy who had come over to the revolution.

One thing is clear, in all the most authoritative accounts of the history of Cuba there was no system of workers' control and management in the classical sense of the term, as understood by Marxists. This is what Carlos Franqui says of the situation at the beginning:

*"Instead of a new society created from below by the workers, Cuba would be a society in which the workers were a productive force obedient to the dictates of those in power. The prime movers of this new society would be Fidel, ten **comandantes**, and the members of the old Communist party.*

"A fusion of the Russian model and the new dictatorial militarism of Fidel Castro was taking place. In a casual conversation with him, one in which I expressed my concern with the course of events, he made a statement that shook me to the core: 'Only the old Communists and the Soviets know anything about communism. We must be patient and learn from them.' I said I knew the Cuban Communists better than he, and that they knew nothing at all about communism. I told him they were unpopular, that the people did not consider them revolutionary, and that they had joined forces with Batista. They fought against the revolution of 1930, had ruined the labour movement, had denounced Moncada, had rejected the Sierra campaign and the clandestine war, and had thrown in their lot with tyranny. Fidel agreed with what I said but insisted that Cuba needed the Communists and would learn from them. I told him to watch out for the second-line Communists, the younger ones of the Prague-Mexico group, including Anibal Escalante and Isidoro Malmierca, because they were Stalinists with strong ties to Moscow. Fidel insisted that in a revolutionary situation it often turned out that the people were not ready and that a revolutionary minority had to take it upon itself to impose socialism on the people. This was an apology for Stalinism. I could see it coming, and there was no way out.

"But what could the people see? They saw the revolution nationalising property, expropriating foreign-owned industries. They saw the old order disappearing and Cuba recovering national independence and dignity. They could also see the heavy

hand of the CIA and the capitalists organising expeditions outside the country. The workers supported as best they could their own unions and knew the charges brought against the union leadership were false. The only thing the unions were guilty of was not being militant Communists, which was a fact, since the unions derived from the Auténtico and Ortodoxo parties, themselves the result of the 1930 revolution that Batista had destroyed. Why the revolution had begun to devour its own children, the working class, was a mystery." [70]

He goes on to recount an argument in the Presidential Palace between Raúl Castro and himself, with Che Guevara present. This exchange is very revealing.

"'You're an anti-Soviet,' Raúl repeated [to Franqui].

"'Look, Raúl, if the Russians really were Soviets, I would be with them. The Party liquidated the Soviets right off the bat. Your problem is that you think that bureaucracy and Soviet mean the same thing. The other thing is that you love Stalin, the man who was the enemy of the people, the new tsar who killed thousands of Bolsheviks and millions of innocent people.'

"Raúl shouted me down: 'Nobody offends Stalin when I'm around!'

"'Really? Listen, Raúl, when I was in Moscow the first time I called him a motherfucker right in his mausoleum in front of the Russians themselves. I'll do it again for you, right here, if you like.' Now he went crazy, foaming at the mouth, shouting his head off.

"Dorticós, [then Cuban President, and later to commit suicide when he was precipitately removed by Castro from his position] ever the clever lawyer, stepped in. 'This gentleman is a Trotskyite,' he said. I denied it, but added that he could call me an anti-Stalinist anytime he liked. I went on to say that I never kept my feelings secret, as did some persons I could mention, and that I had told Fidel himself how I felt about Stalin, power, bureaucracy, and repression in the Miguel Schultz prison. I would be glad, I said, to talk about the invasion and occupation of Poland, Budapest, and Prague if they cared to.

"'Well, suppose we put you up against the wall? History would absolve us,' said Raúl.

"'History absolved us when we rose up against Batista, but now that you're in power and can kill like a Batista, you'll find that you'll be condemning yourself, just as Batista did. So save your threats,' I answered.

"'I'll shoot you right here and now!'

"I ripped open my shirt and shouted, 'Start shooting if you know how!' (Don't think I didn't see the comic side of all this histrionic bullshit. But I was having fun.)

"Then Raúl calmed down...

"I began to feel ridiculous. Then Aleida March said she was leaving because she didn't like people ganged up on like that. Dorticós tried his Trotsky ploy one more

time, so I turned to him and said, 'This isn't my first violent argument with Raúl, but I have no intention of arguing with people like you, who were not even in the revolution.' His jowls began to tremble, and that reminded me of Camilo Cienfuegos's laughter when he talked about people like Dorticós or Augusto Martínez Sanchez and their trembling jowls when they were afraid.

"Dorticós, white with rage, fell into rhetoric. 'You, sir, are offending the office of the presidency.'

"'The only person being offended here is me' was my answer." [71]

Here we have Franqui, an important participant in the revolution, confused but highly suspicious of the bureaucratisation taking place, searching to check this through democracy. In the magazine he was producing at the time he published articles by, amongst others, Trotsky. This and his suspicion of the growing bureaucratic elite earned him the epithet of 'Trotskyite' from Dorticós. This is the ultimate 'crime' in the book of the bureaucracy, which through figures like Dorticós and the privileged officialdom that he represented was developing in Cuba at this time. How is it possible to ignore or pass over in silence these revelations? The sneers of Dorticós, a figure who never fought in the revolution but yet personified the rise of the bureaucracy, signify what was taking place in Cuba at this stage. Was it a misunderstanding, an unfortunate choice of words? On the contrary, in politics language is in general not accidental, especially where the vital interests of classes or castes are involved. 'Trotsky' and 'Trotskyism' are synonymous for every ruling class and for every bureaucratic group on the planet with the threat to their rule by a conscious working class.

Even if a healthy workers' state had been established in Cuba and then the revolution had not succeeded in spreading internationally, particularly to Central America or South America as a whole, an inevitable degeneration would have set in. But as we have seen almost from the outset the Cuban government ruled through the newly merged Communist Party in the Committees for the Defence of the Revolution. They were, in effect, a top-down method of tapping support from the working class.

Tad Szulc makes the following point (in writing his book he discussed extensively with Castro) about the CDRs:

"Full-time security services, however, were not considered sufficient, and on 28 September, the day he came back from New York, Castro announced the creation of Committees for the Defence of Revolution (CDR) as a people's system of collective vigilance. The CDRs were Castro's invention – nothing on such a scale exists even in the Soviet Union – and their immediate function was to keep the police and security

*services informed of strangers appearing in their neighbourhoods (there is a CDR for every urban block and in every plant and farm), citizens voicing criticisms of the regime and so on. Castro estimated in 1986 that 80 per cent of the population belonged to the CDRs, an **unparalleled security network** [our emphasis]. And nowadays the CDRs are also responsible for the vaccination of children and other community tasks."* [72]

Lorimer in answer to our criticism on the role of the CDRs states:

*"Taaffe seems to be unaware that the CDRs were set up to carry out a **repressive function** – to organise the mass of workers and peasants to (as their name implies) repress counter-revolutionary activity – sabotage and terrorism."* [73]

Trying to face both ways he also states a few pages later:

"Between 1974 and 1976, utilising the CDRs as a basis, these representative institutions of workers' democracy were created on the local, city, provincial and national levels – the Organs of People's Power. These are not legislative bodies on the parliamentary model, but working bodies that combine legislative and administrative functions. They are the same type of representative institutions as the early Russian soviets." [74]

Lorimer has absolutely no understanding of the way that institutions which are set up with popular support and approval and which are mainly used against capitalist counter-revolution can, with a change in the situation – increased bureaucratisation – be turned into their opposite as a weapon against Marxists, socialists and communist critics of a bureaucratic regime. The Cheka, the security wing of Bolshevik power, was initially used to defend workers' democracy and to repress bourgeois counter-revolution. However, while retaining the outward forms from this heroic period the security police turned into its opposite as the armed samurai of the Stalinist counter-revolution. It was used in changed circumstances to repress those standing for workers' democracy and the original aims of the revolution.

The Repression of Writers

Of course, the CDRs, even in Cuba today, bear no comparison to the NKVD or the GPU but part of their 'repressive' role is not just against capitalist counter-revolutionaries but those who criticise the Castro regime from the left, demand more freedom, an opening up and a searching for the ideas of workers' democracy. This is just another example of the DSP's cynical cover-up of the increased bureaucratism of the Fidel Castro government. The same applies to their completely abstract attempt to convince us that real workers' democracy existed through the initiatives taken in 1974 and 1978. Lorimer argues that Castro is the modern equivalent of Lenin. Would Lenin have reconciled himself to the Russian Stalinist regime and its publications? Pravda, originally the Bolsheviks' revolutionary newspaper, had been converted by the bureaucracy into a mouthpiece used to justify every crime of Stalin and the Stalinists against the working class. Yet in 1968, after Brezhnev had replaced Khrushchev four years before, Castro, on a visit to the USSR, *"stated in all seriousness that 'Pravda' was the best newspaper in the world"!*[75] Lorimer scandalously tries to excuse the persecution of poets, novelists and others sympathetic to the revolution. Tad Szulc gives an abundance of information on the repression of this layer from 1969 to the mid-1970s and beyond. He states:

"In 1970 the most prestigious Cuban novelists and poets suddenly discovered that without explanation no publishing house or magazine would publish their work. This mysterious ban would last until the mid-1970s." [76]

Lorimer comes forward with what is in effect a further apology for the repression meted out to Herberto Padilla in March 1971. Here we have a former Trotskyist organisation justifying Padilla's 'self-criticism' which comes straight from the Stalinist school of self-abasement. Tad Szulc further declares:

"Castro evidently approved of the crackdown on Cuban intellectuals because the arrest of the poet Herberto Padilla in March 1971 had to have been authorised by him. The arrest led an impressive group of European and Latin American intellectuals, including Sartre and García Márquez, to write to Castro demanding Padilla's release. He was freed 37 days later, after reading a statement of self-criticism and urging other writers to do likewise. His friends regarded him as a 'traitor', but Padilla remained in Cuba for a decade working as at translator of foreign literature. He finally left in 1981, after García Márquez had made another personal appeal to his friend Fidel. Even the obedient UNEAC [Cuban writers association] protested in a letter to Castro the lengthy detention of homosexuals in the military forced-labour units, and they were finally sprung. Yet it left an ugly scar on Cuban society." [77]

The DSP claim that the Padilla incident was 'unfortunate' but has not been repeated since and this shows the openness, as well as the literary and cultural freedom that still exists in Cuba. Tad Szulc answers this:

"Overall Castro's oppressive cultural policies have dealt a lethal blow to creativity in his country; even in 1986 the island was a wasteland of ideas beneath a reign of strict self-censorship. It may take generations for Cuba to return to the free cultural age of José Martí." [78]

The same superficial approach is shown by Lorimer when he examines the alleged 'workers' democracy' and 'people's power' which he claims exists in Cuba.

This is a reference to the so-called 'institutionalisation' of the revolution, as Castro called it, through the introduction of a new Cuban constitution on the 24 February 1976. Again Tad Szulc comments:

"Over the previous 17 years the Fundamental law drafted immediately after victory by the first revolutionary government and literally thousands of laws and regulations had formed the judicial framework of the Cuban state – though no doubt ever existed as to where actual power reposed." [79]

In other words Castro and his group wielded the power notwithstanding any laws passed.

A nationwide discussion took place over the constitution which proposed the creation of a *"popular power structure of local self-government capped by a national assembly"* with legislative functions described as *"the supreme organ of state power"*. There were differences over the method of election of deputies to the national assembly between advocates of direct elections and those favouring choices being made by the *"municipal assemblies of popular power"*. Direct elections in theory would allow a voice in the decision-making process, whereas in the second case nominations from municipal assemblies for membership in the national assembly could, in the Cuban situation, be determined through political manipulation on a local level with candidates nominated. The original draft also provided for national assembly deputies to explain the policy of the state and periodically render account [to the electors]. But that could have been *"disastrous for the central government"* said Szulc, especially if direct elections were introduced. The clash was so great over this issue that in the popular referendum on 15 February 1976 no mention was made of the method of election. Szulc comments:

*"Only **after** 97.7 per cent of the voters had approved the charter did the Central Preparatory Commission headed by Fidel Castro insert the provision that 'The National Assembly... is composed of deputies elected by the Municipal Assemblies'. This was the end of the first and last major attempt to democratise Cuban Marxism."* [80]

In the constitution Cuba was defined as a *"socialist state of workers and peasants and all other manual and intellectual workers"*, with the Communist Party being the *"highest leading force of the society and of the state, which organises and guides the common effort towards the goals of the construction of socialism and progress towards communist society"*. It also hailed Jose Marti who *"led us to the people's revolutionary victory"*, then Fidel Castro under whose leadership the *"triumphant revolution was to be carried forward"*. Again Tad Szulc comments:

"Thus enshrined in the constitutional text Castro was, in effect, named leader for life as a matter of law; the corollary was that it would be unconstitutional (and not just

'counter-revolutionary') to challenge him. Pursuant to constitutional provisions, the National Assembly then elected a 31-member Council of State, including Fidel Castro as its president and Raúl Castro as first vice-president. As president of the Council, Castro became the 'Head of State and Head of Government'. Total power was therefore legally vested in him as President of Cuba and Chairman of the Council of Ministers as well as First Secretary of the Communist Party and military Commander-in-Chief." [81]

Raúl Castro as 'First Vice-President and General of the Army' was automatically designated as his brother's successor. Fidel Castro *"remarked once in absolute seriousness, the creation of the institutions has assured the continuity of the revolu-tion" after his death. He added straight-facedly that he was not really needed any more, explaining that Raúl was his successor (automatically because he had the leadership qualities – not because he was his brother)".* Szulc goes on to comment:

"By 1986, after two more quinquennial congresses of the Communist Party, everything had remained the same, with Fidel Castro the only and final author and arbiter of every decision taken in Cuba. The National Assembly held two annual sessions as prescribed by the constitution, but each session lasted only two or three days." [82]

And all of this is designated by Lorimer as equivalent to the state founded by Lenin and Trotsky between 1917 and 1923. Merely to state this shows how muddled are the leaders of the DSP on the issue of workers' democracy. Not just muddled but also extremely dangerous is the confusion and miseducation, which they are responsible for with potentially important revolutionary forces, particularly in Asia.

Is there a Privileged Elite?

L orimer spends pages and pages trying to demonstrate that no elite existed or exists today in Cuba. In fact he contends power was and is exercised by the workers and peasants in the same fashion as in Russia immediately after the revolution. He derisively dismisses the evidence that we furnish for this. He writes:

"Here's the 'evidence' Taaffe cites: '... Even as early as 1963, KS Karol remarks that in one factory he came across an engineer [who] received 17 times the wage of a worker! Moreover, he cites other perks and privileges cornered by the bureaucracy, such as the "high-class" restaurants like "Monseñor" (sic), the "Torre", the "1830", the "Floridita" and others which charge colossal prices for meals. At the CP Party Conference in 1975 a decision was taken to allow Cubans to buy cars – which up till then had been the preserve of party and state officials!' This is all the 'evidence' Taaffe cites to make his case." [83]

Lorimer outlines a liturgy of excuses for the privileges that exist. These amount to the fact that the high-class restaurants were merely for foreign tourists and that all cars prior to 1975 were the preserve of the state. But how does this refute the contention of Karol that this 'state property' was used almost exclusively by the state officialdom? Guevara, who lived a very austere existence, taking even less than the official salary, himself recognised the bureaucratic trend that existed soon after the revolution, never mind today, and was intolerant of anyone in his immediate entourage who demonstrated any such tendencies.

Jon Lee Anderson gives examples of this. He writes:

"Everyone knew that Che had refused to collect the salary he was due as president of the National Bank, and he had continued the practice at the Ministry of Industries, steadfastly drawing only his minuscule comandante's wages. Orlando Borrego, by now a vice-minister, felt obliged to draw only an equivalent amount of his own salary, donating the rest to an agrarian reform fund; it would have been unseemly to be earning more money than his boss. " [84]

Anderson further comments:

"Not all of Che's comrades, including some of his ministerial level peers, appreciated this revolutionary showmanship... When Cuba's wealthy had fled the country, they

*had left behind a huge stockpile of cars, promptly nationalised, which the various government ministries allocated to their officials and certain employees. But Borrego had gone one better. During a visit to an 'intervened' sugar mill a manager had pointed out a brand-new Jaguar sports car that had been abandoned by its owner and suggested that Borrego take it, since no-one else knew how to run it. Borrego fell instantly in love with the car and sped around proudly in it for about a week, until the day he drove into the garage where he and Che parked their cars, and Che spotted him. He came towards him yelling: 'You're a **chulo** – a pimp!'"* [85]

This was one case where the egalitarian Che Guevara could check an individual minister's tendency towards bureaucratism. But this could not, given the relative isolation of the Cuban Revolution and its reliance on Stalinist Russia, prevent the increasingly bureaucratic degeneration overall. Of course, the privileges, as we have commented above, when the lava of revolution had still not cooled, were relatively small, particularly when compared to the luxurious lifestyle of the elite in the Stalinist states of Eastern Europe, Russia and even of China. But privilege was not just expressed in a salary 17 times higher than that of a worker – which Lorimer just passes over as one example of one deviation in one factory. It is also shown in the access to 'high-class' restaurants that existed and still exist in Cuba not just for tourists but for the privileged officialdom.

If Lorimer won't accept our evidence or that of Karol then what has he got to say about the conclusions of François Maspero in his introduction to Janette Habel's important book 'Cuba – Revolution in Peril'? Both authors' roots are probably closer to the DSP then to us. Habel is a leading member of the United Secretariat of the Fourth International (USFI). Maspero says he has "rejoined the Fourth International," presumably the USFI, which had illusions about Cuba in the early period of the revolution. Yet this is what he writes:

"Let's face it – there is no point in mincing one's words – democracy does not exist in Cuba. Human rights have not been and are not respected: at the worst moments, the figure of 80,000 political prisoners was reached. And nor are the rights to freedom of information, expression and movement respected." [86]

He also writes in relation to Karol, whose evidence Lorimer dismisses:

"Karol who, with the encouragement of Fidel Castro himself, had written a rigorous analysis of Castroite power that remains today the most honest and complete work of reference on the period, had a taste of [Castro's wrath]. So too did René Dumont, who had talked agronomics and socialism with his usual outspokenness. Both were denounced by Fidel Castro as agents of the CIA, before a crowd of about 500,000 Cubans – who had heard another story." [87]

The result of offending Castro through his well-documented criticisms resulted in Karol's books and name being banned in Cuba.

Privilege and corruption, which was limited in the early stages, later grew substantially. Habel devotes virtually a whole chapter to the corruption amongst the bureaucracy, which was endemic by the 1980s. This is just a sample of what she found:

"Waste and corruption have led to a feeling of discontent among the regime's base of support, the wage-earning strata, faced with the growing wealth of certain sectors of farmers, as well as the privileges enjoyed by the administrative bureaucracy and top officials of the economic and state apparatus. Signs of economic inefficiency, waste, theft and the misappropriation of goods have been joined by the black market and currency trafficking, the spread of prostitution, and a growth of petty delinquency near tourist centres. All such phenomena had fallen considerably – disappeared, in fact – in the years following the seizure of power.

"From June 1986, the Politburo of the PCC undertook an 'exhaustive analysis of the problem of crime and anti-social behaviour', particularly in Havana, highlighting 'instances of aggressive conduct, violence against the person, and "hooliganism" displayed in the capital'."

Habel continues:

"Just over a year later several top officials fled to the United States, either by using considerable resources in foreign currency which they had embezzled or by taking advantage of special facilities, thus pointing to the importance of certain privileges. In 1986 Manuel Sánchez Pérez, vice-minister in charge of purchasing technical supplies from abroad, deserted to Spain with US$499,000. According to his declarations, 'While still in Cuba I did some business deals with foreign firms and accumulated funds for the purpose of creating [abroad] an institution which will prepare a strategy for a return to democracy in Cuba'. This gives some idea of the facilities available to leading officials. In May 1987, General Rafael del Pino, a former fighter at Playa Girón, managed to reach the United States in a small Cessna 402 aeroplane, taking off from an airbase with his wife and three children 'under the pretext of taking a trip round the island'. The mind boggles at the ease with which this general had access to a private runway. "

Habel concludes:

"In June 1987, Luis Domínguez, the president of the Institute of Civil Aviation (INA), was arrested, accused of corruption and the misappropriation of resources; he supposedly had personal bank accounts to the tune of $500,000. This arrest was followed by the desertion of Commander Florentino Aspillaga Lombard, the head of Cuban counter-espionage in Czechoslovakia,[88] and then by that of Gustavo Pérez Cortt,

vice-president of the State Committee for Technical and Material Supplies (CEANT), in January 1988...

"This desertion of top officials was a symptom of the exacerbation of social and political tensions, particularly amongst the most privileged strata who felt insecure and threatened by the current direction taken by Castro. Corruption, the misappropriation of funds from enterprises or using the latter for private ends have been repeatedly denounced...

*"During the twenty-fifth anniversary of the Bay of Pigs in April 1986, the offensive was resumed 'against those who confuse income from work and speculation, fiddlers who are little better than thieves, and indeed are often thieves.' This theme reappeared during the CTC [trade union federation] Congress: denunciation of the huge profits made, thanks to the existence of a significant private sector, by the **nouveaux riches** (truck owners, farmers, middlemen in charge of selling works of art, etc); by administrators linked to external trade or enjoying privileges gained in trips to Western countries (also denounced by the Young Communists at their 1987 congress); by 'bureaucrats with comfortable homes'; and by technocrats who build 'two huge nickel-processing factories and only provide accommodation for the manager and the thirty or forty top cadres, while the workers are put up in makeshift huts'."* [89]

The Bureaucracy and the Workers

Condemnation of 'bureaucratism' is nothing new for Castro or other leading figures of the state or government. But, writes Habel, *"From 1965, commissions had been charged with the rationalisation of surplus administrative staff...There is no comparison between what was being denounced then and the current situation. The 1970s were a decade in which the Soviet Union regained a dominant influence in all areas – institutional, political, economic and ideological; and this dominance, followed by the introduction of the economic reforms, gave further impetus to the spread of bureaucratisation in a country where basic goods are still rationed."* [90]

After dismissing the evidence of Karol, Lorimer then goes on to quote Robert Scheer and Maurice Zeitlin who base their analysis on personal observation. In their book, 'Cuba: An American Tragedy' they give a fairly balanced account of the first stages of the revolution. But Franqui gave a timely warning to writers visiting Cuba even in the early days after the revolution's triumph:

"For progressive people it is easy to see oppression in the capitalist world. It was against that oppression that we rebelled in Cuba – the same sort that filled jails in Franco's Spain, that makes the black ghettos of New York a hell, that hides Rio's misery at carnival time. But people should also open their eyes to the crimes that

make socialism as it is practised in the world into the negation of the ideal of social-
ism. My advice to travellers is not to confuse what you see with what actually exists.
Try to look beyond." [91]

It is advice which Lorimer and the DSP should heed today.

Nevertheless, Scheer and Zeitlin are honest observers of the Cuban Revolution in
its first decade and although displaying in part a certain idealisation and romanti-
cism about the situation in Cuba, they do show that the extent of privilege was very
limited in the first period of the revolution:

"It was a rare administrator who earned more than the highest paid skilled worker
in the same factory. Typical administrators earned the low salary of $350 a month;
many earned no more than $250. The administrators in some factories were formerly
skilled workers in the same plants. Their salaries were relatively low, not only because
Che, the minister of industries, believed in this as a socialist principle, but also
because wages were frozen and administrators received the same salaries they earned
in their preceding jobs. Some of them did enjoy certain material 'fringe' benefits: a car,
for instance, if their work required one." [92]

This, however, does not invalidate the point that we have made that the extent of
the privileges of the as yet unconsolidated bureaucracy were very low, and could
not be otherwise, in the first stages of the revolution. But even then the officials in
the new state could acquire certain 'luxuries', which did include access to a car as
we have seen, which were not open to the masses.

Moreover, on the basis of the growth of industry a differentiation between the
mass of the population and a growing bureaucracy opened up and inevitably would
widen where control and management was not exercised over the state and society
by the workers and poor peasants. Indeed Zeitlin shows clearly the absence of real
workers' democracy in this first period of the revolution. He writes:

"The members of the government, the cabinet ministers, are responsible not to the
general citizenry – who did not elect them and who had no direct voice in their
selection – but only to themselves and a handful of revolutionary leaders – Fidel, Raúl,
Che, – who appointed them. These leaders are, in fact, the government. They are the
decision-makers; and there are no established channels by which the masses can
directly influence them or recall them. (One must not forget on the other hand that the
people are armed; wherever one goes, one sees ordinary citizens, including long-
fingernailed women in high heels, with rifles or submachine guns slung over their
shoulders. If this is not an institutional mode of ensuring responsibility of govern-
ment figures, it is, nevertheless, a certain source of countervailing power.)" [93]

Yes, there was a 'countervailing power' at the beginning in the militias and the elements of workers' control that existed but these alone were not, and are not, sufficient to check the growth of a bureaucratic elite. Zeitlin further writes:

"[The revolutionary leaders] failed to attempt to create autonomous centres of power outside the Party that could act to check and balance the Party's strength. They apparently made no attempt to establish new autonomous institutions to protect dissent and prevent infringements on personal freedom." [94]

He makes the same point about the role and independence of the trade unions in a workers' state. Guevara, in a discussion with Zeitlin, defended the right of workers to strike and was of the opinion that,

"Strikes stem from the malpractice of those in charge at all levels of industry, and that strikes while - certainly not to be encouraged – are a necessary working class weapon to be used when other methods fail." [95]

Thus, instinctively, Guevara understood the need for genuine trade unions in a workers' state to be both a supporter of 'their' state and at the same time a defence of the working class against the abuse of this very same state. But the leaders of many of the trade unions did not share Guevara's approach, as Jesus Sotu, organisational secretary of the central labour organisation, and another member of the union's central executive committee and editor of its journal, showed in a discussion with Zeitlin.

"Neither seemed to have even an elementary Leninist conception of the labour unions' role as defenders against 'bureaucratic deformation' in a 'Socialist society'. Both stressed the unions' functions of raising the productivity of the workers... [but] neither mentioned that a union ought also to protect the immediate interests of the workers". [96]

Later, Zeitlin, in 'Cuba's Workers, Workers' Cuba, 1969', a new introduction to his 'Revolutionary Politics and the Cuban Working Class', gives his own impressions of Cuba at that time. Lorimer draws heavily on this account in order to refute what we say above about the existence of a bureaucratic elite. Zeitlin, he says, proves that not only was there not a bureaucracy "from the outset" but such an elite did not exist even as late as 1969. Cuba, he maintains, for the first decade of the revolution had, in effect, a regime of 'war communism', similar to the period of the civil war following the Russian Revolution. Not only did 'war communism' exist but the regime in Cuba, as we have seen, was the same, he claims, as that of Lenin and Trotsky, basically a healthy workers' state with mild bureaucratic deformations.

However, Zeitlin's material was based on his personal observations in Cuba.

Many of his comments are valuable in showing the support of the mass of the working class and rural population for the Cuban Revolution even in the teeth of the great difficulties experienced in the 1960s. His comments about the attitudes of different layers of the working class – not all of them unqualified supporters of Castro or the political regime that existed – are useful in helping to form a picture of Cuba at that time. He states:

"The egalitarian ethos of the revolution has been accentuated by its egalitarian practice."

He goes on to point out:
"Wages and salaries reflect the same pattern of social equality." [97]

He gives the example, quoted by Lorimer, of a factory employing 2,700 workers where the administrator earned $250 a month. A section chief earned $400 monthly. Skilled workers earned, in effect $300 a month, while the lowest *peón*, or unskilled worker, earned about $95 a month. But even if these figures of official salaries are accurate they do not give the full picture. We have conceded, both in our original pamphlet and in this reply to Lorimer, that given the stage of the revolution, its cultural level, during the 1960s there could not be the same kind of differentiation between the bureaucracy and the masses as existed at that stage in Eastern Europe and the former Soviet Union, for instance. However, even Zeitlin cautiously suggests that there were other privileges:

"There are certain limited perquisites of office. Many government functionaries have drivers and cars assigned to them for use on government business, mostly four-cylinder compact Volgas or Alfa Romeos, though an occasional Chevy or Ford still serves the revolutionary government....

"Functionaries, especially those dealing directly with foreign visitors, also have expense accounts which allow them to indulge more often than other Cubans in meals at the few remaining plush restaurants frequented still by the wealthy who have chosen not to leave. Public property, and accessible to all, such restaurants are a luxury few Cubans can yet afford."

Zeitlin writes:
"From what I could observe... expropriated country homes...[did not become] the opulent quarters of a new elite." [98]

This is frankly contradicted by Carlos Franqui who writes:
"At that time [in 1961] Security was moving comandantes, ministers and anyone of any importance into new houses. Some of us tried to stay where we were – Che, Faustino, Celia, Haydée, Chomón, Orlando Blanco, and I among them. The new

houses were those that had been abandoned by the Havana middle class. This reopened the polemic that had been simmering since 1959. Many of us went right back to our old apartments after the war while others wanted to 'profane' (as they said) the houses of the rich. It was they who were 'profaned'. These houses came equipped with 24-hour, round-the-clock guards – because of the counter-revolutionary threat, but it was also a good way to keep an eye on you in the Soviet style. Celia, Haydée, and I had eluded the new-house situation simply because we were civilians... I had been living in my own flat all this time with no problem".[99]

However, the premises in which Franqui's newspaper 'Revolución' was produced had been mysteriously attacked a few months earlier. He suspected it was not so much right-wing, counter-revolutionary terrorists but the burgeoning Stalinist 'security' forces that targeted him because of his criticism of the bureaucratic degeneration of the revolution. He writes:

"Since I wouldn't obey the order to move, Fidel stepped in, told me I was in danger and that I would simply have to follow orders. The next day the Urban Reform people handed me the keys to my new house. I'd be a hypocrite if I were to say I didn't like what I found – swimming pool, books, nice furniture, garden, air conditioning – but at the same time I felt guilty. Fidel himself never had those problems, since he was accustomed to living in houses like that...What was really happening was that we were creating a new elite, despite all the rhetoric about the need to protect us, the need for upper-echelon people to be able to relax. This new elite would one day be dangerous." [100]

Let us remind ourselves that these events occurred in 1961 not 1969 when Zeitlin recorded his impressions.

Notwithstanding the honesty of Zeitlin, Franqui's observations are a more accurate account of what was taking place in Cuba. As a participant in the revolution, as a friend and confidant of the leaders of the revolution but also as a stringent and honest critic of elitism and bureaucratism, as well as Stalinism, he was better placed to give a more rounded out view of what was taking place in Cuba. Nevertheless, Zeitlin's analysis actually speaks against Lorimer's contention that Cuba had all the features of a healthy workers' state at that stage. Referring to the trade unions, for instance, he writes:

*"From what I could observe, and from the vague and infrequent references to them by the workers I interviewed, they seemed to have 'withered away'. The workers do not have an **independent organisation** which takes the initiative in the plant, industry, or country as a whole, to assure, let alone demand, improved working conditions or higher wages; no organisation exists as an autonomous force to protect and advance the immediate interests of the workers, as they see them, independent of the prevail-*

ing line of the Communist Party or policies of the Revolutionary Government. The distinction in practice between the role played by the Ministry of Labour and that of the CTC-R, the Workers' Federation – if it is clear in formal terms – is not clear to ordinary workers. Nor, indeed does this distinction seem clear to some of the government officials and national leaders I spoke with. " [101]

No Soviets

He further comments: *"The unions function essentially, however, less as workers' independent organisations than as committees delegated by the workers to represent them on a day-to-day level concerning working conditions, as well as to provide for the distribution of scarce resources to the workers on a fair basis."* [102]

As to overall control of society, the economy, the factories, etc., Zeitlin comments: *"The distinction between the Party, Workers' Councils, general assembly, and the union as a means of furthering their interests has become vague in [workers'] minds."* [103]

In relation to the danger of bureaucracy, Zeitlin bluntly writes:
"The possibility exists that under the social pressures of what Che called the 'weeds that shoot up so easily in the fertilised soil of state subsidisation,' of vested interests that may emerge (risen careerists, bureaucrats, and political opportunists), and of some members of the old privileged strata incorporated into positions of authority in the economic administration, government, or Party, the thrust towards social equality clearly evident at present could be subtly, even unconsciously, deflected." [104]

He points out that Lenin and Trotsky were both in favour of the workers having the freedom to organise to protect their immediate interests. Independent unions should act both as a defence of a healthy workers' state and also as a defence of the workers against 'their' own state. Most important are Zeitlin's comments about the overall management of society and the economy:
*"At present, despite the apparently ample participation of the workers in discussions and decisions concerning the **implementation** of the objectives of the national economic plan set for their plant, the workers have no role whatsoever, to my knowledge, in determining the plan itself. They have nothing to say over investment priorities; the decision as to what and how much is to be produced is made by the central planning bodies of the Revolutionary Government responsible to the Council of Ministers."* [105]

He also points out that as opposed to the days of the revolution when *"genuine differences between government leaders were still publicly debated, if in muted tones"* the situation in 1969 was that *"public debate is absent"*. Moreover, in relation to the Escalante affair in early 1968 (see my pamphlet on Cuba where this is explained), he validates the points that I made rather than the uncritical position of Lorimer towards this. In relation to the trial of the so-called 'micro-factionists' led by Aníbal Escalante, former organisational secretary of the PSP, he writes:

*"Several of the government's charges were sufficiently vague to encompass even **pro**revolutionary dissent from the present policies of the Revolutionary Government".*

He goes on to point out:

*"The charges are essentially that Escalante and his comrades differed with the Revolutionary Government's policies and attempted to convince others of their views. They were accused of 'furthering ideological differences' in the Party, despite the fact that 'on numerous occasions' several of them had been 'called in to discuss their **ideas** and **attitudes** which were opposed to the line of the Revolution'."*[106]

His conclusions are:

"To say the least, this trial might have had a chilling effect on the expression of opposing views even within the Central Committee itself, and in the country at large amongst revolutionary cadres; and it sets a precedent for the imprisonment of revolutionaries who deviate from the party line."

Zeitlin points out:

"Once 'attitudes, ideas and arguments' can lead to imprisonment, the potential for the repression of any or all who express competing views, even the most loyal revolutionaries, has been established. It is good, but not enough, to say as Fidel did after the trial, that 'the revolutionary courts were not as severe as some would have wished, but in the final analysis unnecessary severity has never been a characteristic of this revolution'."[107]

It is beyond question that soviets existed in Russia in the period leading up to the revolution and the immediate period afterwards. They were weakened because of the civil war, which saw the flower of the proletariat deployed in defending the revolution against the armed attacks of imperialism. The proletariat itself became almost atomised, as Lenin commented, because of the civil war and the extreme privations that this introduced. However, it was still legitimate to describe the state at this stage as a relatively healthy workers' state. Power was wielded by the most revolutionary party in history and, it might be added, the most democratic. The leaders of this state, notably Lenin, Trotsky and the Bolsheviks, were conscious of the inherent dangers of bureaucratisation that flowed from the isolation of the revolution. They therefore took measures to try to prevent and hold back the process. In Cuba, however, there were never any 'soviets' in the classical Marxist sense of the term. The leaders of the revolution, moreover, did not have a consciously worked-out programme or perspective and as we have seen were compelled to turn towards the bureaucracy of the 'Communist' party and remnants of the old state machine. Therefore the situation was entirely different in Cuba compared to Russia between 1917 and 1923.

Sad to say our old friend Karol, summarily dismissed by Lorimer, is much more accurate on the issue of workers' democracy, soviets and the lack of them in Cuba than the ex-Trotskyists of the DSP. His comments on the situation in Cuba are more penetrating on the general issue of the transition from capitalism to socialism than the DSP leadership. He makes the following insightful comments:

"Fidel Castro will often tell you: it is five times more difficult to develop a country after the revolution than to seize power. He does not hesitate to illustrate this thesis by the example of his own practical errors, all due to his lack of experience. But this is not really the point. The reason it is five times more difficult to build a socialist society than to seize power is the failure to create a genuine socialist outlook even while the struggle is still being waged, or to establish popular methods of running the new society. Socialism has no chance of success unless, in the very fire of action, at the very point of social explosion, a move is made towards the solution of the delicate problem of the relationship between the masses and the political leadership. Now the search for this solution was never part of the Castroist scheme. True, without Fidel, Cuba would be like the Dominican Republic, but this does not alter the fact that Fidel's method – the only possible one, perhaps – is the basic cause of his greatest difficulties. A people that says: 'If Fidel is socialist, so are we' is not really mature enough to build a socialist society; it has only just been admitted to the rank of builder's apprentice." [108]

We would dispute Karol's contention that Fidel's method is *"the only possible one – perhaps"*. But his general point about the consciousness of the working class and socialism is valid. Karol comments on the early debates following the victory of the revolution amongst the leadership:

"In this whole debate there was a major gap which genuine Marxists might have been expected to close. Neither Che nor his opponents have come to grips with the problems of political power in, and the political organisation of, all those societies where centralised or reformist experiments in planning and economic management were taking place. The 'classics' which both sides so assiduously quoted, had never equated socialism with mere economic efficiency; ie, with economic control by a small group deciding, in the name of the people, on the best way of organising work and leisure. One can look in vain to Marx for this concept of permanently delegated political and economic authority. On the contrary, for Marx the entire transition period

towards socialism and communism was characterised by the direct participation of all workers, free at last in the running of communal affairs. Even for Lenin, the founder of the theory of the proletarian vanguard party, Soviet power still came before electrical power." [109]

On the issue of 'direct democracy', an idea formulated in relation to Cuba by the US left intellectuals C. Wright Mills and Paul Baran, Karol comments:

"Castroists did not still pretend that direct democracy, based on a dialogue between Fidel and the rank and file, constituted an end in itself and not just a step towards a genuine workers' democracy. Far from trying to develop 'a system of more organic relations between the rightful government and the Cuban people' they tell themselves that this system already exists, indeed that it appeared in 1959-60 and that it has proved its worth ever since." [110]

Karol's conclusion is:

"The building of socialism cannot be the business of one man or of a single group of men, however well-intentioned. If the socialist ship is to come safely into harbour, everyone alike must take to his oars – a few men rowing up in front are not enough. This may sound like a slogan, but socialist democracy is not the kind of luxury people can only afford when everything else has been settled. Unless everyone pulls his weight, the leaders no less than the workers are exposed to an intolerable strain. In such circumstances, it matters little that great sacrifices no longer serve to enrich a minority of privileged people, or that the leaders are men of high integrity – and no one can say otherwise of the Castroists. The result is bound to be apathy and a general flagging of political interest." [111]

These lines are not particularly scientific but they express more horse sense about the reality of Cuba, both yesterday and today, than those of Lorimer.

In coming to the conclusion that a bureaucratic elite dominates Cuban society we do not base ourselves exclusively on the individual observations of this or that commentator but on an analysis of the processes which are likely to develop following a revolution that is isolated, particularly in a relatively undeveloped country like Cuba. And we do not start with a blank sheet. We can call upon the accumulated experience of the Russian Revolution and its subsequent development, including the bureaucratic degeneration that flowed from its isolation as we explained earlier. It does not even occur to Lorimer to ask the question that even if, as he contends, a relatively healthy workers' state was created in Cuba in 1959 to 1960 how is it possible that it has maintained itself intact for over 30 years? Has it remained a healthy workers' state without spreading internationally, particularly to the industrialised countries, and without experiencing the bureaucratic degeneration which Russia went through after 1923? If so is this because of the revolutionary intransigence of Castro and his entourage, including the Cuban Communist Party? This is pure idealism, which ignores the colossal heritage that Trotsky has left us in his analysis of the objective causes of the bureaucratic degeneration of the Russian Revolution.

Let us nail here a gross misrepresentation of our position where Lorimer accuses us of trying to show: *"Castro is a Cuban Stalin"*.[112] This is despite the fact that he uses quotes from our pamphlet, which clearly show we do not believe that Castro could be put in the same box as Stalin. Stalin was a grey mediocre figure who played no significant role in the Russian Revolution, who developed into a tyrant and was perfectly fitted, as Trotsky pointed out, to head the bureaucratic counter-revolution which eliminated the Bolshevik party and established the bureaucratic regime. Castro was a revolutionary, without having a rounded-out Marxist understanding or programme. He demonstrated enormous combativity, improvisation and originality in the struggle against the Batista regime. To his credit he also reflected the huge pressure of the masses in the period of the revolution to break with capitalism and establish a planned economy. Given the character of the Cuban Revolution, and the fact that Castro and the 26 July Movement originated outside of a Stalinist tradition, as well as reflecting the traditions of Cuba itself, the regime which was established did not and could not initially ape all the features of the regimes of Eastern Europe, Russia or China. The situation in Cuba was much more fluid. We argued in our pamphlet, that there was not just massive popular support for the revolution but elements of workers' control in the factories and on the farms. However, this does not in itself constitute what Marxists would consider a healthy workers' state. Even in Yugoslavia under Tito there was an element of workers' control in the factories as the bureaucracy attempted to tap the initiative of the masses to extricate the planned economy from the impasse caused by the bureaucratic caste which controlled industry and society.

Once more Habel provides some interesting detail on this issue. She writes about the situation in Cuba:

*"A hierarchical approach can be found, to a greater or lesser degree, in all sectors of society, to the point where enterprise managers are often called **el jefe** (chief). The latter's privileges and power in relation to the workers are clear. In 1983, a trade union activist – the social affairs secretary of the light industry rank-and-file section and an attender of the sessions of the **consejos de trabajo** (work councils) – challenged the absenteeism of particular managers and asked the council to deal with the issue. 'The administration was reluctant. I said: "I can prove that of the 24 administrators' time*

*cards in this workplace, 18 showed unjustified absences." But still the management balked at bringing a case. I tried other routes. I talked to the union, but the union would not back me up. It was just too hard for the union leaders to force the issue because it meant going against the **jefes**. The situation was never resolved. The* **consejo** *could never do anything at all'."* [113]

She also points out:

"Workers' councils were set up in 1965 to rule on problems of indiscipline and violations of labour law in enterprises. They can only be formed by workers. According to the law of 1965, they were to be composed of five members elected by secret ballot at their workplace for a three-year renewable period. They are charged with the resolution of conflicts between workers and managers over discipline and workers' rights. They mainly deal with conflicts over absenteeism, late arrival at work, the failure to follow tasks, carelessness, the lack of respect for managers, instances of physical assault, damage to tools, as well as cases of fraud and robbery. But wages, working conditions and transfers also form part of their responsibilities." [114]

She points to the role of Guevara in this:

"Set up on Che's initiative, the councils were initially independent bodies formed by the workers themselves. They had real power to control, even though the scope of their activities was limited by the overall low level of training at the beginning of the revolution. In the recent period it is significant that lack of time has been one of the councils' major problems. The number of conflicts has become increasingly large and the councils have been criticised for not managing to deal with them. To cope, workers had to add this task to their ordinary work, hence the trend towards the councils' decline. The problem could have been solved by a cut in the working hours, but intensification of work was the order of the day." [115]

Decision Making

On the crucial issue of the overall management of the economy, Habel quotes Francis Pisani: *"With infinite patience **compañero** Gada [the manager] explains the principle of what could be called the 'yo-yo economy' to me. This consists of sending figures, suggestions or demands 'upwards' and waiting for answers, directions and orders to come back 'downwards', in an endless to-ing and fro-ing between the rank and file and the leadership. It is extraordinarily difficult to locate the level at which decisions are taken, even though the correct answer is always to say 'above', but without saying from where."* [116]

From all the most authoritative accounts, Hugh Thomas's 'Cuba or The Pursuit of

Freedom', or Jon Lee Anderson's biography, 'Che Guevara', a picture emerges of the character of the Castro leadership in the first stages of the revolution. This is a leadership that is driven empirically and very courageously to establish a planned economy but with no real power vested in organisations controlled and managed by the mass of the population themselves. A high degree of personal power was in the hands of Castro, Guevara and the leading group in the first period. Decisions were taken on the basis of personal intervention of Castro and others rather than through representative organisations of the masses themselves. This is what Tad Szulc said about Castro's role:

"His compulsive dedication to detail and the conviction that, no matter what the subject, he knows more about it than anyone else, have combined to make Castro an obstacle to an efficient development of both economy and society... Therefore, a mutually protective association of bureaucrats has come into being, and the bitter Havana joke is that Cuba does have a two-party system after all: the Communist Party and the Bureaucracy Party. The waste of resources and talent is staggering." [117]

And later he adds:

"His impatience led him into continuous shifts between short-, medium- and long-term planning as well as into endless improvisations. No policy was given reasonable time to succeed (or to be proved unsatisfactory), and political or visionary pressures pushed Castro into grandiose projects the economy could not possibly handle." [118]

Habel writes:

"In 1970 a Cuban intellectual was already lucidly denouncing the even further concentration of power in Fidel Castro's hands. He stressed the need for the participation of the masses and the different social groups in economic and political decisions, as opposed to the impossibility of managing from a single centre. But he was already expressing doubts as to the likelihood of this occurring:

'I am a bit pessimistic as to the likelihood of such changes coming about. I would like to be wrong, but Fidel's own words show that his idea is to provoke a few changes of individual people, solve a few minor problems irritating the masses, and win popularity through a few personal visits and conversations at workplaces. But as you can understand, that won't change anything and it's inconceivable that such measures might lead to a reactivation of the economy and to the masses retaining confidence in the leadership'." [119]

Pisani illustrates the limited scope for workers in decision making:

"In one small enterprise 75 out of 300 came to the assembly. As to the self-critical attitude of officials, one activist says that it is the case of the well-known technique of pre-empting the accusations to come. Although all issues are dealt with, including the

failure to meet targets set by the plan, few young people participate and there is an overwhelming atmosphere of weariness. Two days earlier, a production assembly had discussed the same issues, and, during the course of the second assembly, a worker summarises the situation well: 'We know what the problems are. Now we'd like to know how to solve them.'"[120]

Habel concludes:

"This is a good summary of the more general problems affecting Cuba: debate and criticism are open, but this 'eiderdown democracy' does not give any power to those practising it." [121]

It is true that this situation was tolerated, if you like was acquiesced to, by the mass of the population of Cuba, particularly as the framework of a planned economy was established. On this basis Cuba was therefore able to introduce significant improvements in health, education and social services, many of which generally exist today, and compare particularly favourably to the conditions in many of the neighbouring Latin American countries. There were important aspects of the Cuban Revolution and of the regime that arose from it, which were different to the heavily bureaucratised regimes of Eastern Europe and the former Soviet Union. The regime was not an exact copy of the Stalinist regimes of Eastern Europe, Russia or China. There were features in Cuba that did not exist in those societies. This could not fail to be the case given the character of the revolution and how the new state was established.

Marxists need to recognise the differences that exist between different states. The enduring popularity of Castro's regime was evident in the first and subsequent period. But it is also necessary to note the fundamental similarity in the economy and in the state forms which began to evolve in Cuba, particularly when Castro was forced to lean on the Russian Stalinists. Given the blockade exercised by US imperialism the Cuban regime turned towards the Stalinist regime of Russia.

In the first stage of the revolution Castro was reaffirming his commitments to the US, to foreign investment in Cuba, insisting that his agrarian reform law would affect only neglected land. He urged more US tourism and he expressed his hopes that the United States, Cuba's biggest sugar buyer, would increase Cuba's sugar quota. He also said that Cuba would

"Honour its mutual defence treaty with the United States and continue to allow the US Navy to use the Guantánamo base – and while it may come as a surprise to those in the know back in Havana, he was also opposed to Communism and in favour of a free press". [122]

This underlines once more how facile and impressionistic is Lorimer's contention that Castro was a conscious Marxist prior to the revolution. He was feeling his way, as was the Russian bureaucracy. It took events, the attempted blackmail of Cuba and the imposition of a blockade, to radicalise Castro, to bring to an end the temporising which he showed immediately after the revolution. And yes, let us restate again 'under mass pressure' he carried through step by step the expropriation of landlordism and capitalism. This represented a colossal step forward both for the Cuban people and for the downtrodden masses in the Latin American continent and throughout the neo-colonial world.

However, Khrushchev, representative of the Russian bureaucracy par excellence, had no interest in spreading genuine socialism to the rest of the world. A healthy workers' state, based upon workers' democracy, represented a deadly threat to the Stalinist bureaucracy as much as to world imperialism. However regimes which assumed the economic and political forms of Russia itself, a planned economy but without workers' democracy, the Russian bureaucracy would find not only compatible but also useful in its military-diplomatic manoeuvres against American imperialism.

The support for the Cuban regime, despite Khrushchev's statements about support for 'socialist states', had everything to do with extending the power, prestige and world position of the Stalinist bureaucracy of Russia and nothing to do with genuine international revolution. This was subsequently shown in the Cuban missile crisis when Cuba was used as a pawn in the manoeuvrings against US imperialism. The US had established nuclear bases in Turkey and Khrushchev's answer was to install them in Cuba. Of course the Cuban regime wished to have a shield against attack from US imperialism but this was of secondary importance to Khrushchev, whose policy was determined by the national interests of the Stalinist bureaucracy and not out of concern for the workers and peasants of Cuba or of Latin America as a whole.

Trotsky's writings on Stalinism represent an even greater contribution to our understanding of revolution, of social counter-revolution and of the world we live in today than his participation in the Russian revolution. Trotsky's 'fall from power', subsequently viewed with astonishment by superficial bourgeois commentators, had nothing to do with his personal qualities or lack of them but was the result of an objective process, given the isolation of the revolution. Trotsky himself, in view of his enormous authority with the Red Army, could have taken power and removed Stalin. But as he himself commented, this would have meant he would have been a prisoner of a military bureaucratic caste, which in some senses could have been worse, at least in the first period, than the bureaucratic 'civilian' layer who supported Stalin. He also commented that Krupskaya in 1927 said that if Lenin had lived he would have been in prison because of the bureaucratic degeneration. The process of bureaucratism is inevitable, as Trotsky explained, on the basis of a paucity of cultural and economic resources. Russia, even with the resources of a continent at its disposal, faced inevitable bureaucratic degeneration on the basis of its isolation.

In the words of Marx, where 'want is generalised, all the old crap will revive'. First and foremost the state would not only continue to exist but grow in a society of scarcity and poverty. The bureaucrat forced to regulate and preside over the rationing of resources ensures that 'he eats first and eats best'. The isolation of the Russian Revolution led to the discouragement of the masses, their elbowing aside and the gradual rise of a bureaucratic officialdom. To begin with their conditions were not all that better than the mass of the population. But gradually the power and the privileges and income that go with it were concentrated in the hands of this stratum, personified by the rise of Stalin. Such a process is inevitable on the basis of the isolation of a revolution. The origins of the Cuban Revolution were different than those of the Russian Revolution but the processes of bureaucratic deformation and degeneration were fundamentally the same.

Foreign Policy

Abig part of Lorimer's criticism of our position concerns the international effects of the revolution and the foreign policy of the Cuban state. The Cuban Revolution had a big effect worldwide but particularly on the countries of Latin America. There was tremendous sympathy and support amongst the downtrodden.

However, its effects were entirely different to that of the Russian Revolution. There was great sympathy amongst the masses in Latin America, throughout the neo-colonial world, and amongst the more conscious layers in the labour movement in the developed industrial world. But in the case of the Russian Revolution, the working class outside of Russia understood that their class had come to power, had established democratic soviets and a state, which enshrined workers' rule for the first time in history. There was no similar response, nor could there be, in the case of the Cuban Revolution because of the class forces involved.

The riposte of Doug Lorimer to this is to simply assert that the 'Castro leadership has always stressed the need to mobilise the peasants and the workers'. Yet, even in this phrase, the DSP puts the same emphasis as the Castro leadership: 'The peasants and the workers.' Lorimer does not pose the question which both Guevara and Castro did as to which class was primary and which secondary in the revolution.

Guevara was clear in his article, 'Cuba: Historical Exception or Vanguard of the Anti-Colonialist Struggle?' He dealt with the methods that should be applied to the revolution throughout Latin America. He states:
"The peasant class of America, basing itself on the ideology of the working class, whose great thinkers discovered the social laws governing us, will provide the great liberating army of the future, as it has already done in Cuba." [123]

Dozens of such statements of Guevara and Castro at this time could be quoted to show that in their view it was the peasants, using the methods of guerrilla warfare, through which the revolution would be triumphant. Karol wrote in 1970 that Fidel Castro
"Had told me several times that the Cuban Revolution was not a proletarian revolution". [124]

The working class would play the role of an auxiliary as it had done in the case of the Cuban Revolution. Moreover, Castro and Guevara attempted to put this strategy into practice in Latin America by supporting numerous guerrilla organisations and guerrilla 'foci' in the 1960s. This was a mistaken strategy for Latin America as a whole where the working class was the key revolutionary class, as events were subsequently to demonstrate in Argentina, Brazil, Chile, Uruguay and many other countries in the continent.

A correct approach would have involved a revolutionary appeal, a mobilisation of the working class in the cities, backed up, in the words of Marx, with a 'second edition of the peasant war',[125] a movement in the countryside of the poor peasants. This is what actually happened in the Russian Revolution, the lessons of which is a book sealed with seven seals for the apologists of guerrilla warfare like the DSP.

But, for the Latin American working class to move from general support for the Cuban Revolution to an active position of seeking to emulate it, Cuba itself would have had to have shown in action that the working class exercised direct control and management of the state and society. This patently was not the case, even in the first period of the revolution, and has become even less so subsequently.

It is true that an enormous impediment existed to a correct revolutionary policy in Latin America in the form of the leadership of the Stalinised Communist Parties in the continent. Nevertheless, a clear revolutionary appeal by a democratic workers' state to emulate the Cuban Revolution would have found a ready response amongst the mass of the working class and the poor peasants despite this leadership. Instead of preparing for the creation of genuine revolutionary parties located, in the first instance, in the urban areas and amongst the working class, guerrilla warfare based upon the peasantry was the chosen method of spreading the example of the Cuban Revolution. Despite the revolutionary integrity of Che Guevara and his heroic efforts to rouse the populations of Latin America, this was a mistaken strategy which Castro was forced to abandon following Che's murder in 1967 in Bolivia and the failure of similar guerrilla movements elsewhere.

France and Mexico

Lenin and Trotsky held that the working class must play the leading role, even if they are in an absolute minority in society, within the revolution. The DSP not only misunderstands this issue when applied to Latin America but, more tragically in a sense, to the movements taking place in Asia and, particularly, the revolution in Indonesia. To them the main revolutionary class is now the 'urban poor', rather than the organised working class. In Indonesia, the urban poor can play an important role but the decisive forces for the revolution lie in the organised working class organised in big industry.[126] A viable revolutionary mass party must first of all find a basis amongst this class as a means of finding a way to the oppressed poor in the urban areas and, of course, of the exploited poor peasant masses themselves. This is not an incidental question or of subjective academic interest. The history of Latin America in the 1970s and 1980s is littered with tragic examples of where the revolutionary potential was ruined by the false methods of guerrilla warfare, in the cities and urban areas as well as in the rural areas. These methods were used in largely urbanised societies such as Argentina, Uruguay and elsewhere.

And what was the role of the DSP and other alleged Marxists and even some 'Trotskyists' when these ill-fated policies resulted in the squandering of the enormous revolutionary potential and of a whole generation? They acted as cheerleaders to the guerrilla organisations – making sure that, in general, the majority didn't personally participate in their actions. This led to the ruination of a whole generation of potentially revolutionary Marxist fighters. Moreover, never have these organisations drawn up a real balance sheet of the baleful effects of their policies and methods. Militant – now the Socialist Party – and the Committee for a Workers' International have had a consistent position of opposition to such methods. We have always adopted the friendliest attitude towards genuine revolutionaries attracted to these mistaken methods. But we have sought to emphasise the role of the working class, and the building of a mass revolutionary party rooted in this class, as the main tasks for Marxists.

On foreign policy, the DSP are also apologists for the Castro government. I criticised in my pamphlet Castro's stance over the massacre of the students in Mexico in October 1968, his position on the greatest general strike in history in France in 1968, and on Czechoslovakia. Lorimer has rushed to excuse the stand of Fidel Castro and in so doing unintentionally bears out our arguments on the character of the Cuban regime. We pointed out that the financial and economic dependence of Cuba on the Stalinist bureaucracy of Khrushchev and that of Brezhnev ultimately determined and shaped the character of the Cuban regime. Lorimer writes, in relation to the Escalante Affair (which we deal with in our pamphlet) that,

"Moscow indicated its displeasure by sharply cutting back its supplies of vitally needed oil to Cuba." [127]

Precisely! In the action taken against Escalante – with the use of completely undemocratic methods it might be added – the Castro government asserted the national position of their regime vis-à-vis the attempts of the Kremlin to convert Cuba into a mere appendage like Eastern Europe. In this struggle, what was at issue were the interests of the Stalinist bureaucratic regime in Russia and the government of Castro. His government was still popular with the mass of the population of Cuba but, nevertheless, it also rested on the bureaucratic elite that controlled the main levers of power and the state in Cuba. As with the clashes between other regimes within the 'Soviet orbit' this was not a conflict between a regime of genuine workers' democracy (Cuba) and the Kremlin bureaucratic regime. The two bureaucracies were asserting their own separate and rival national interests. In the cases of Mexico, France and Czechoslovakia – the Castro government acted to support the Kremlin bureaucracy (Czechoslovakia), or remained silent in the teeth both of the repression in Mexico and the massive workers' movement in France.

And Lorimer and the DSP are unashamed apologists for Castro in the stand that he took. Unbelievably, this is what they write:

"Now, unless Taaffe has information to the contrary, all the available evidence shows that in 1968 there was neither a mass revolutionary party in Mexico or France that could have been disoriented by the Castro leadership's failure to comment on the internal developments in these countries that Taaffe refers to. Does Taaffe actually believe that a message of solidarity to the French students from the UJC (the state-controlled Cuban student movement) or the Cuban Federation of University Students would have changed the outcome of the May-June 1968 worker-student revolt? Does he think that a public protest by the Castro leadership against the 1968 Tlatelolco massacre in Mexico would have led to the overthrow and replacement of the PRI government by a revolutionary government? If he does believe either of these things then he is vastly more out of touch with reality than even his hyperbolic description of the impact of the May-June 1968 events in France would indicate." [128]

It is interesting that Lorimer finds our characterisation of the May-June 1968 general strike in France as 'hyperbolic' (grossly exaggerated). Can we assume from this that the DSP did not believe that this was one of the greatest movements of the working class ever in history? That a revolutionary situation existed in France at that stage? If they answer in the negative, it would show that they understand as little about the French events as they do about developments in Cuba and the character of its regime. What is astonishing in their apologia for the Castro leadership is that they justify the silence of Castro on the massacre of the flower of the Mexican youth in 1968 and on the French events on the basis that it would not have made any 'difference' because no mass revolutionary party existed. It is shameful for a 'Marxist' organisation to argue in this fashion.

The justification for their stand is the following:

"What would have been the most likely outcome if the Castro leadership had acted

*as Taaffe thinks it should have? A statement of protest against the Mexican govern-ment's repression of the student demonstrations would have most likely have result-ed in a change in the Mexican government's policy – not towards the Mexican student movement, but toward Cuba! When the hangman's noose of the US imperialist blockade was being tightened around Cuba, the Mexican bourgeois government resist-ed Washington's pressure to join the blockade and refused to break off diplomatic and trade relations. Mexico was the **only** country in Latin America that maintained relations with revolutionary Cuba. In that context, the Castro leadership has not made any criticisms of the Mexican government."* [129]

Thus the reasoning of the DSP is that the parlous economic and diplomatic situation of Cuba means that the Castro government is compelled to remain silent in the teeth of repression of a section of the world workers' or youth movement. The same applies when a unique revolutionary situation such as France exists which, if it had succeeded, would have transformed the situation of the working class worldwide, including that of Cuba itself.

This is a million miles removed from the position of the Bolsheviks, the regime of Lenin and Trotsky between 1918-21, when Russia faced not just an economic blockade but the military intervention of the 21 armies of imperialism. When movements of the working class took place, when revolutions developed in Germany, Czechoslovakia and in Italy in 1920, for example, the Bolsheviks intervened and openly advocated support. The Russian government also sought to buy time by combining military resistance to imperialism with diplomatic manoeu-vres, the purpose of which was to divide one imperialist power against another. With the ending of the civil war, the diplomatic efforts of the Bolsheviks were an important arm of its foreign policy. But at no time did this take priority over the Bolsheviks' attempts to assist all revolutionary movements worldwide.

It would have been inconceivable for Lenin or Trotsky to have allowed any diplomatic or other short-term state interests to over-ride the need to support workers in struggle, never mind support for revolutions. For instance, when Chicherin, a leading Bolshevik representative in London, came under pressure in his diplomatic dealings with the British imperialists, he suggested to Lenin that in order to arrive at agreement with them certain 'democratic' changes should be effected in the Soviet constitution. Lenin suggested politely that he should be ignored!

Support for workers in other countries did not always come from the government itself, but from the Russian and other Communist parties. If Castro feared the breaking-off of relations with Mexico then the government itself would not necessarily have had to take an official position. But what was to stop the Cuban Communist Party, or the student wing of the Communist Party, or the trade unions, which in a healthy workers' state would be semi-independent at least, from condemning the slaughter of the Mexican students? Merely to pose the question in this way shows how shallow is the apologia of the DSP for the Castro leadership. This was not the last time that Castro acted to bolster the Mexican bourgeoisie. In the summer of 1988 Castro personally attended the inauguration of Mexican President Salinas (usually diplomats represented Cuba abroad). Salinas had been declared elected through widespread ballot rigging and the general opinion was that the opposition candidate Cárdenas should have won. Habel comments:

"The Mexican left felt betrayed by the personal presence of the figure [Castro] embodying the Cuban Revolution." [130]

The same applies to the May-June events in France in 1968. The workers occupied the factories in the greatest general strike in history and the threat of revolution hung over France. No less a figure than De Gaulle vindicated this point when he fled to Baden-Baden in Germany – believing that the 'game was up' – in order to prepare for a march of the French army of the Rhine against a revolutionary France. He had reckoned without the perfidious leaders of the French Communist Party and Socialist movement at the time, who derailed this revolutionary opportunity into the safe channels of parliamentary elections.

Does Lorimer agree with the French CP leadership that to characterise this as a revolutionary opportunity was 'hyperbolic'? If so, he supports those who sabotaged, or let slip, one of the greatest opportunities for the working class to transform not just France but Europe and the world by completing what the workers had started in those heroic months.

Czechoslovakia

In relation to Czechoslovakia, we read one of the most astounding, not to say disgraceful, apologies for Castro's support for the crushing of the Czechoslovak spring in 1968. In answer to our arguments, Lorimer declares:

"What does Taaffe think would have happened to Cuba's vital supplies of food, oil, machinery and weapons if Castro had denounced the Soviet invasion of Czechoslovakia? How does he think Moscow would have reacted if Castro had not given verbal support for its sending of 350,000 troops into Czechoslovakia? The security of Stalinist rule there was obviously of far more importance to the bureaucrats in Moscow than the fate of Escalante's little group in Cuba (and the Kremlin indicated

its displeasure over the Castro leadership's attitude over Escalante by sharply reducing vital supplies of oil to Cuba in early 1968)."[131]

So, once more, after deriding our contention that the Castro regime was economically and militarily reliant on the beneficent Kremlin bureaucracy, which ultimately shaped the character of the regime, we now have Lorimer and the DSP vindicating our analysis. They go, however, a lot further in arguing that Castro, the head of a 'healthy workers' state', remember, based on workers' democracy according to the DSP, had 'no choice' but to support the Kremlin's repressive action in Czechoslovakia. But what are the implications of this incredible statement? Prior to 1989, if a healthy workers' state had developed in a relatively small country then it would have had no choice, in foreign policy at least, but to have avoided denunciation or criticism of the counter-revolutionary role of the Kremlin bureaucracy on a world scale. This is the shameful muddle that the DSP has got itself into because they have abandoned the principled Trotskyist/Marxist approach towards the struggles of the working class internationally.

There is not an atom of internationalism in their approach. Contrast their position to that of Lenin who stated baldly that if a choice was to be made between maintaining the Russian Revolution or guaranteeing the success of the German revolution, then the Bolsheviks, would have no hesitation in plumping for the victory of the Germany revolution as the priority. If necessary, he argued, this might have meant temporarily sacrificing the Russian Revolution in order to gain the victory of the German workers. The impact of a successful German revolution, particularly on Western Europe, would have been greater than even the Russian Revolution itself. This in turn would have speeded up the prospect of world revolution.

Ultimately, the fate of Cuba rested on the shoulders of the world working class, and not in the Kremlin. This was clearly demonstrated in a negative way after the collapse of the Berlin Wall when the Russian capitalist governments of Gorbachev and Yeltsin unceremoniously pulled the plug on the Cuban economy and the Castro regime. In effect, the DSP and Lorimer are justifying Castro's stand over the Czechoslovak events. They vehemently deny that Castro was uncritical and give long quotes from a speech by Castro at the time to underline this. But what does Castro actually say? In the very speech which Castro made on 23 August 1968, quoted by Lorimer, Castro hints that what he might say could be *"in contradiction with our own interests... and they will constitute a serious risk to our country"*. He then goes on to say:

"In our opinion, the decision concerning Czechoslovakia can only be explained from the political point of view and not from a legal point of view. Not the slightest trace of legality exists. Frankly, none whatsoever."

These and a few other asides are sufficient for Lorimer to declare:

"Castro's declaration on the Soviet invasion of Czechoslovakia was thus not one of uncritical support. In fact, it was so critical of the policies of the Stalinist regimes in Eastern Europe and the Soviet Union that none of them reprinted it." [132]

But Castro's speech clearly supported the intervention. This is what Castro stated, according to Lorimer:

"We had no doubt that the political situation in Czechoslovakia was deteriorating and going downhill on its way back to capitalism and that it was inexorably going to fall into the arms of imperialism." [133]

He then goes on to state bluntly:

"We acknowledge the bitter necessity that called for the sending of those forces into Czechoslovakia; we do not condemn the socialist countries that made that decision." [134]

A number of asides were made by Castro about the Kremlin adopting a 'consistent' position but, ultimately, bluntly stated by Castro, he supported the Kremlin's suppression of the Prague Spring with massive military might.

There was no serious threat of a return back to capitalism in August 1968 in Czechoslovakia. At bottom, the struggle was between the mighty centralised Russian bureaucracy and the liberal nationalist bureaucracy of Czechoslovakia, represented by Dubcek. The movement overwhelmingly accepted the planned economy but there was a clamour amongst the masses for democracy and liberalisation. There were some elements in the movement who, even then, looked towards the market, a return back to capitalism, but the overwhelming majority of the mass of the population stood for the maintenance of the planned economy but with democratic 'reforms'; 'socialism with a human face'.

Czechoslovakia, and particularly the leadership of Dubcek and Co, was not as threatening to the Kremlin as the Hungarian Revolution had been twelve years before. The Hungarian commune, as we have commented earlier, represented a deadly threat to the Stalinist bureaucracy everywhere. Its workers' councils, with all the elements of workers' democracy, called forth the panicky opposition not just of Khrushchev and Andropov (of the KGB) in the Kremlin, but of the 'liberal' Tito in Yugoslavia and Mao Zedong and Zhou Enlai in China. There could be no compromise with the Hungarian Revolution. In Czechoslovakia, on the other hand, the movement had not gone as far with Dubcek representing a Czechoslovak version of the movement that coalesced behind Gomulka in Poland in 1956. Gomulka represented the Polish nationalist bureaucracy, which in 1956 sought and achieved the loosening of the grip of the Moscow bureaucracy. Against the background of the Hungarian Revolution the Russian Stalinists were prepared to accept Polish 'independence' because Gomulka did not threaten the rule of the bureaucracy either in Poland or in Moscow. This was a clash of a rising nationalist bureaucracy with the Kremlin oligarchy in a similar fashion to Czechoslovakia in 1968. In 1956 in Poland, the Kremlin was forced to come to terms with Gomulka and accept the independence of the Polish bureaucracy.

The situation was entirely different in Czechoslovakia because of the changed situation in Eastern Europe, in Russia itself and worldwide. To have granted independence to the Czechoslovak 'liberal' bureaucracy then, even with the mainte-nance of the planned economy, threatened to speed up the centrifugal forces of disintegration that were present and which we saw at the end of the 1980s in Eastern Europe. An independent Czechoslovakia – even one that maintained the bureaucratic rule, but 'liberalised' under the regime of Dubcek – would have immediately detonated movements in the neighbouring countries of Hungary, given a colossal push to the anti-bureaucratic opposition in Poland, and possibly would have led, decades earlier, to the downfall of Ceaucescu. Not least would have been its impact on the radicalised workers and youth in Western Europe and the USA, etc. It was a movement of earthshaking proportions, which the Kremlin believed they had no alternative but to crush. And the DSP and Lorimer, in effect, seek to apologise for the apologists of this Stalinist crime.

The crushing of the Czechoslovak 'experiment' marked a turning point in Eastern Europe, as did the suppression of the Solidarity movement of 1980-81 in Poland (which was also supported by Castro). It played into the hands of capitalism worldwide in further discrediting 'socialism', which was now identified with tanks, guns and aeroplanes being used to suppress a movement for democracy. It also reinforced the pro-market tendencies within the Czechoslovak dissident movement which, with the further disintegration of Stalinism in the 1970s and 1980s, led to the collapse of the regimes of Eastern Europe and of Stalinism. This led to a return back to capitalism with all that this has meant for the struggles of the working class internationally. It is absolutely incredible that any organisation claiming to be 'Marxist', never mind Trotskyist, could adopt the kind of position that Lorimer sets out.

He also berates me for my comments on the attempts of the Cuban regime to seek agreements with the US capitalists as a means of lifting the economic blockade of the island. Unfortunately for Lorimer, most informed commentators agree with us. Cuba's relationship with different US administrations points to the fact that the

Castro government sought to arrive at a diplomatic understanding starting with the Kennedy administration itself, which had only just previously attempted to overthrow Castro through the Bay of Pigs invasion. Jon Lee Anderson states:

"He and President Kennedy had been edging toward a behind-the-scenes détente, sending exploratory messages back and forth with a view to 'normalising' relations, when Kennedy was assassinated in Dallas."

Following Kennedy's assassination and his replacement by Johnson,
"Fidel was sending a clear signal that he hoped the new American President, Lyndon Johnson, would resume the abruptly severed initiative." [135]

Angola, Ethiopia and Nicaragua

Lorimer also castigates me for writing in my 1978 pamphlet:
"The Carter administration is prepared to recognise the Cuban regime once it abandons its intervention in the African continent." [136]

He says:
"That is the sum-total of what Taaffe has to say about Cuba's sending of 20,000 troops in late 1975 to help the newly independent government of the former Portuguese colony of Angola to repulse a US-backed invasion of that country by South Africa." [137]

Lorimer demonstrates that he has no sense of proportion. He lashes me for not dealing fully with Cuba's involvement in Angola. To have written a book but not mentioned Cuban support for Angola in some detail would have been a serious omission. But he himself notes that my pamphlet was the compilation of three relatively short articles. This could not deal extensively with the reasons for Cuba's support of Angola against the intervention of South African imperialism. Nevertheless, we will take the opportunity here of explaining the reasons for Cuba's intervention in Southern Africa. And, I'm afraid, that this does not coincide with the one-sided views of Lorimer and the DSP.

He contrasts the Cuban intervention in Africa in 1975 to the
"Stalinist bureaucrats in Moscow, Beijing and Belgrade [who] never used their armies in the way the Cubans used theirs in Angola. The Stalinists used their armies as border guards to defend the base of their institutionalised privileges." [138]

This is an entirely superficial way of posing the issue. We have never denied that the Cuban Revolution evoked enormous enthusiasm on the part of the Cuban masses (300,000 Cubans volunteered to fight), which generated an earnest desire on their part to spread the revolution internationally. The idea of carrying the example of Cuba to Latin America and the rest of the neo-colonial world affected not just the working class and the poor peasantry, but also sections of the bureaucracy itself. Nor, by the way, was this unique to Cuba. Even in Moscow, Beijing, Vietnam and elsewhere, the bureaucracy was able to tap the support for workers internationally in order to justify their foreign interventions. Sections of the bureaucracy also wished to see the victory of 'socialism', ie the establishment of societies similar to their own with a planned economy but one-party totalitarian regimes.

Even Stalin prior to 1933, as Trotsky pointed out, wished to see the victory of the German revolution. Only after the victory of Hitler and the Nazis – a terrible defeat for the world working class – did the bureaucracy begin to fully crystallise into a caste, which then dreaded the victory of the working class anywhere. In the long run, support for a bureaucratic form of 'socialism' had the purpose of defending their 'institutionalised privileges'.

There was enthusiasm amongst workers in Russia for that country's 'intervention' in Spain in the 1930s, which was presented by Stalin and the bureaucracy, of course, as an example of 'internationalism'. There were a huge number of Russians who volunteered to fight in Spain. They were affected by the hot flames of the Spanish Revolution. They were such a source of revolutionary contagion in Russia itself that Stalin butchered most of them on their return to Russia in the purge trials of 1937-38. Anybody who had been connected with an international workers' revolution was suspect in the eyes of Stalin and the bureaucracy, partly because they would have become a rallying point in the first stages of a political revolution against the bureaucracy itself.

The intervention of the Chinese army in Korea was not just a question of them being 'border guards'. The Chinese masses were raised to a revolutionary fervour in opposition to the intervention of imperialism in its attempt to hold back the tide of revolution in the region and Asia as a whole. Even the intervention in Afghanistan in 1980 – supported uncritically by the DSP –initially had the support of significant sections of the Russian people. Opposition only developed as the body bags of Russian conscripts began to come home and it dawned on the Russian people that military intervention was largely to protect the strategic and military interests of the Russian state and the privileged elite that dominated it.

The intervention of Cuban troops in Angola in 1975 arose from a combination of reasons. There was undoubtedly great sympathy for the Angolans amongst the

Cuban masses. This was also linked to the worldwide sympathy of the masses for the struggle against the South African apartheid regime. Tad Szulc argues that it was Fidel Castro's idea, not the Russians, to engage Cuban combat troops in the Angolan civil war *"on an absolutely open-ended basis"*. Initially Stalinist Russia withdrew its support for the MPLA, not trusting it politically and militarily, and *"leaving Castro as its only friend"*. However with the Cuban military intervention Soviet arms belatedly began arriving through Brazzaville in early October 1975. Later that month the South African apartheid regime, through 'Operation Zulu', entered with considerable force into Angola. Cuba replied with a huge airlift of troops, 'Operation Carlota'. This intervention undoubtedly saved the MPLA regime and helped it to defeat its enemies in the crucial battle for the railway terminal of Benguela on 5 November, and assured its capture of the capital, Luanda – threatened by Holden Roberto's FNLA – in time for Angolan independence on 11 November.

In the next decade 200,000 troops were rotated in the Cuban intervention into the Angolan civil war. Does this represent an example, as Lorimer argues, of a clear, principled, international working-class approach? From the mass of the Cuban people, from even sections of the Cuban bureaucracy itself also, there was as we have explained an earnest desire to prevent an outright apartheid, counter-revolutionary victory in this region. Castro himself had personal ties with the leaders of the MPLA who had spent some time in Havana prior to 1974. At the same time, despite their hesitation at first, as Tad Szulc has again argued: *"In Angola, and later in Ethiopia Cuban and Soviet interests have coincided."* [139] Without the acquiescence of the Russian Stalinist regime Castro would not have been able to intervene in the way that he did, given the colossal financial and military dependency of Cuba on Russia. By the mid-1970s Cuba was receiving about one-half of total Soviet economic aid to all of the Third World (including Vietnam) as well as probably one-half of Soviet military aid to these countries.

Moreover it is one thing for Cuba to have assisted a similar 'Third World' revolution; it would have been an entirely different situation if a genuine revolution had unfolded elsewhere with the working class in full control. At the same time, the interests of the Russian bureaucracy were at stake in Southern Africa. The regime of the MPLA in Angola, in the aftermath of the withdrawal of the Portuguese imperialists, had moved significantly along the road to break with landlordism and capitalism. This regime economically and diplomatically inevitably moved into the orbit of Moscow, as did Mozambique.

The revolutionary upheavals that had convulsed both countries from 1974 onwards worried the South African imperialist ruling class. The movements in

Angola and Mozambique already exercised a profound effect within South Africa itself, shown later in the Soweto uprisings of 1976. South African imperialism, therefore, supported every attempt to overthrow the regimes of Angola and Mozambique, including supporting opposition movements such as the pro-Western UNITA in Angola. They decided in 1975 to intervene to assist in a military overthrow of the MPLA. This had the tacit support of the major world imperialist powers of Britain and the US. To allow this to have taken place without any resistance would have represented a severe blow to the military, strategic and diplomatic interests of the Russian bureaucracy worldwide, but particularly in the neo-colonial world where it still competed ferociously for support against American imperialism.

On the other hand, the direct intervention of Russian troops would have provoked an immediate response from US imperialism. Moreover, the intervention of 'white' troops – albeit Russians in the uniform of the 'Red Army' – would not have been tactically adroit, particularly as there was the alternative of Cuba, closely allied to Russia and with a significant 'Third World' and black population. Of course, this intervention roused and inspired the Cuban masses whose soldiers fought and sacrificed heroically for what they perceived was their internationalist duty. To say that is one thing. To argue that this intervention alone demonstrates an unswerving revolutionary internationalism of the Castro regime akin to that of the Bolsheviks is naïve in the extreme.

If the Cuban leadership, what Lorimer calls the 'Cuban Communist Party', were consistently international revolutionists, why the entirely different approach adopted towards the Nicaraguan Revolution? Here was a movement, the Sandinistas, which had been inspired by the Cuban model. One of the leaders, Tomas Borge, had visited Cuba in the first period after the revolution and had discussed with Che Guevara. The Nicaraguan Revolution, however, did not imitate the Cuban Revolution.

It was not classical guerrilla warfare rooted in the countryside, but had more of the character of a mass insurrectionary movement in the cities and countryside – something similar to the Spanish Civil War. Under the pressure of the revolution, the Sandinistas were compelled to take over 40% of industry and big sections of the land. However, the revolution was not completed, and Castro, together with the Russian bureaucracy, played a large part in ensuring that this was not so.

In 1985, faced with the threat of an armed counter-revolutionary military intervention backed by US imperialism, the Sandinista leaders flirted with the idea of 'doing a Cuba'. In April, Sandinista leader Daniel Ortega visited Moscow to discuss getting the support of the Soviet Union. By this time, the Russian bureaucracy had moved into active opposition to the establishment in the neo-colonial world of new deformed workers' states. They were seeking more and more an accommodation with imperialism – Cuba had shown the heavy price economically which would be called upon Russia if similar regimes were established in the neo-colonial world. Therefore, they actively discouraged the Sandinista leaders from going down the road trodden by Castro and Guevara 16 years before. Tony Saunois makes the following comment in his pamphlet on Che Guevara:

"Castro dutifully supported his paymasters [the Kremlin bureaucracy] and put pressure on the FSLN leaders. A small number of Soviet MiGs destined for Nicaragua were impounded in Havana. He had previously visited Managua in January 1985 to urge the FSLN to support a mixed economy, telling them: 'You can have a capitalist economy,' and praised Ortega for his 'serious and responsible approach'." [140]

Why does Lorimer not take up this statement from an important CWI publication, moreover one that was produced in the recent period? How do Lorimer and the DSP explain the difference between Castro's attitude ten years previously in relation to Angola and the position adopted in 1985 in relation to Nicaragua? We look forward to their explanation, which, no doubt, will be the same kind of so-called 'realpolitik' that Lorimer has employed already.

The present situation in Nicaragua, which arose from the failure to complete the revolution and the refusal to spread it to the rest of Central America and South America, is the responsibility not just of the leadership of the FSLN in Nicaragua. The Kremlin bureaucracy, of course, carries a huge responsibility, as does Castro who was at one with his 'paymasters' and also, we have to say, so are Lorimer and the DSP. In Lorimer's long treatise there is not one line about Nicaragua and the role of Castro. At least I did mention the situation in Africa in my original articles and pamphlet. This is just one example of the leadership of the DSP's double book-keeping.

Lorimer writes:

"Taaffe deals so sparingly with the Cuban role in Angola because it provides conclusive evidence that his 'analysis' of the Castro leadership is 100 per cent wrong. His inability to recognise the proletarian revolutionary character of that leadership is testimony to his sectarian inability to **practice** *– as opposed to merely talking (and lecturing others) about – the art of revolutionary politics."* [141]

We believe we have answered Lorimer on the issue of the Cuban intervention in Angola. We will pose another question to Lorimer relevant to the issue. Was Castro acting in a 'proletarian revolutionary' manner in supporting the regime of Mengistu in Ethiopia? The Derg, the government of Ethiopia led by Mengistu, had presided over the elimination of the feudal regime of Haile Selassie, and taken significant steps along the road to a break with landlordism and capitalism. At the same time, there was not an atom of 'democracy', either bourgeois or 'workers', in the Ethiopian regime. Moreover, it was suppressing the legitimate national democratic rights of the Eritreans and other oppressed nations within Ethiopia.

At bottom, the same factors were present, which were used to justify Cuban intervention as in Angola. The Ethiopian regime rested economically and even militarily on Stalinist Russia. There was a convergence between the interests of Cuba, particularly of the drive of Castro to enhance his reputation as a 'Third World' leader and revolutionary, and the strategic and military interests in the Horn of Africa of the Russian Stalinist bureaucracy. Again as Tad Szulc comments: *"In Third World policies, Castro and the Russians were totally on the same wavelength"*.[142] The presence of Soviet-supported Cuban forces in the crucial Horn of Africa nearly led the Carter administration in the USA to break off Strategic Arms Limitation Talks with the Soviet Union.

Castro with Peruvian president Fujimori, Havana

Cuba's Future

One of the most bankrupt assertions of Lorimer and the DSP is the claim that we, and other socialists and Marxists, have no right to issue the slightest criticism of organisations and their leadership in Cuba or the neo-colonial areas of the world because we happen to live in the developed industrial countries. This is a complete rejection of real internationalism. The CWI has a presence in 34 different countries on every continent. Some of our organisations are sizeable parties with significant influence amongst workers, while others are relatively small groups. Does Lorimer's embargo on commenting on and criticising workers' struggles extend to all of these sections or is it just restricted to Marxists who live in the industrialised countries? The success or failure of the workers' movement in any part of the world is vital to workers' struggles elsewhere. It is not only the right but also the duty for genuine Marxists to discuss and criticise each other's strategy and tactics employed in the struggle to overthrow capitalism and establish socialism.

This is how Trotsky approached the question in the 1930s. Prior to Hitler coming to power he pointed out that the key to the international situation was the struggle of the German workers, then it was France, and then it was, of course, the epic struggle of the Spanish workers culminating in the civil war. In the most friendly, comradely fashion, Trotsky and the International Left Opposition offered their views, unfortunately not accepted in most cases, as to how the revolution should be prosecuted to a successful conclusion. The defeat of the movements in Germany and Spain affected the world working class.

The Cuban workers have every right to criticise our struggles in Britain, including the strategy and tactics we employ. We would hope to learn from the criticism of workers and organisations in any part of the world in the battle that we are waging in Britain. Unfortunately, on the basis of Lorimer's attack on us on Cuba, there is absolutely nothing to learn in the school of the DSP. Indeed, to follow their approach, their methods, their tactics and their policies would be disastrous.

Unlike the DSP, we have a record of leading successful mass struggles of the working class in Britain: in the Liverpool battle between 1983-87 and in the mighty anti-poll tax campaign. We might also add that we played a key role in the struggle against the fascist BNP in Britain and the closure of its headquarters in south

London. This does not mean that we are automatically 'right' on all issues. Whether we are correct or not has to be established in discussion and debate. It is an indication of the puerile tail-endism of the DSP that this issue is even raised by them. They attempt to profit from the tremendous sympathy that exists for the Cuban Revolution and its achievements.

They do this by distorting the character of the Cuban regime, by excusing the mistaken policies of Castro and his government, and by glossing over and covering up for the real bureaucratic degeneration which has taken place in the Cuban state.

Nor do they deal anywhere with the damage that has been inflicted on Cuba by the bureaucratic bungling and the constant zigzags in policy, which have undermined the great advantages of the planned economy. Castro's policies, the Cuban equivalent of the 'war communism' of the Bolsheviks, were carried not just for a few years but for a whole decade in Cuba. The utopianism of Castro involved the nationalisation of hot dog stands, of small businesses and an attempt to do away with 'money'. We have commented on the deleterious effects of this on Cuba and will not repeat it here.

But the DSP have particularly objected to our analysis which compared Castro's policies in this period, particularly in 1968, to what happened in China during the 'Cultural Revolution'. The scale of disruption, bloodshed and convulsions was enormous in China. After all, the 'Cultural Revolution' affected one-quarter of humankind, and therefore was of colossal proportions. Similar methods in a nation of ten million would not have the same consequences. The regime of Mao was much more brutal than that of Castro for a number of reasons that we cannot go into here. But our analogy still retains its validity and is moreover underlined by Tad Szulc:

"Castro proclaimed a new radical revolution in Cuba, which in a sense was his equivalent of the Chinese Cultural Revolution that was just then beginning to wind down. Although Cuba had no Red Guards and no blood was shed, Fidel moved to nationalise the entire retail trade sector still in private hands – businesses ranging from auto mechanics' repair shops to small stores, cafés and sandwich and ice-cream street vendors – for reasons of ideology. Like Mao Zedong, Castro must have felt that revolutionary fervour was fading amongst his people, and that a powerful injection of radicalism was needed to make the juices flow again. He called his policy the Great Revolutionary Offensive, imposing revolutionary purity by eliminating the remnants of the 'bourgeoisie' he so despised, and mobilising Cuban manpower on a gigantic scale (voluntary extra work by everybody) for agricultural production, and especially the record sugar harvest he was planning for 1970." [143]

Castro denounced an estimated 955 privately owned bars *"making money right and left, consuming supplies"* and linked the number of hot dog stands with the threat of counter-revolution. His battle cry was: *"Are we going to construct socialism, or are we going to construct vending machines?"* [144] He also commented to KS Karol in 1967 that it was *"Absolutely necessary to de-mythicise money and not to rehabilitate it. In fact, we plan to abolish it totally."* [145]

Again, this sheer utopianism is brushed aside by the DSP in their eagerness to cling to the coat tails of Castro. In 1968 Castro had personally taken over the planning and execution of economic policies, shutting off all alternative ideas and naturally *"brooked no arguments"*. Again Szulc declares:

"Fidel had become a total dogmatist, disregarding absolutely the experiences of other men and other societies, and also rejecting many Marxist views... As René Dumont, the French agricultural specialist who was the most perceptive foreign observer of the Cuban scene in the late 1960s, remarked later; 'There was nothing to buy, for which reason there was no stimulus to work'...In Cuba, Castro seemed determined to prove that to go backward in Marxist economic history represented progress." [146]

Without conscious democratic control by the working class, mass discussion, a testing and retesting of plans with the necessary corrections added, even the greatest geniuses in a planned economy will inevitably make the grossest blunders. And Castro was not a genius in the mould of Lenin or Trotsky, despite the arguments of the DSP. Why then, declares Lorimer, was the Cuban regime still popular with the majority of the population? He seems to forget that even the Stalinist regimes of the USSR and Eastern Europe enjoyed a measure of 'popularity' at one stage. The masses tolerated the bureaucracy in the teeth of imperialist threats, so long as the planned economy was maintained and took society forward.

For a period, the Stalinist regimes were still capable of playing a 'relatively progressive' role in developing industry and society. The rate of growth of the Russian economy, for instance, was way beyond that of capitalism as a whole in the 1950s, 1960s and at least part of the 1970s. In roughly the decade and a half leading to 1989 Stalinism became 'an absolute fetter' on the further progress of these societies. The huge military bureaucratic regime had swallowed up more and more of the surplus, was clogging up the pores of society and preventing it from going any further forward. The plan began to disintegrate, the economy and society began to regress. This laid the basis for the upheavals of the 1980s and 1990s in the USSR and Eastern Europe leading to the collapse of the Berlin Wall.

Gains can be preserved through Workers' Democracy

Cuba also reached a turning point in the 1980s. For a quarter of a century before then Castro's Cuba *"was carried by the momentum of the revolution"*. In 1986 far ranging purges of the highest ranks of the Castro regime were carried out. He fired without explanation some of his oldest and closest associates and proclaimed a *"strategic revolutionary offensive"* to *"capture the effervescent fervour"*. Political controls and repression against all forms of dissent were further strengthened, and Cuba went on a war footing as people's militia units were trained and kept on the alert against an American invasion Castro insisted was imminent. Yet, the economy continued to stagnate with not enough sugar being produced to meet export commitments to the Soviet Union. There was even the appearance of unemployment, which was partially dissipated by the Cuban soldiers serving abroad and by hundreds of thousands fleeing into exile.

This situation was compounded by the collapse of the Soviet Union that plunged Cuba into an acute economic crisis, enormously aggravated by the stepped-up attempts of US imperialism to isolate Cuba through its brutal arms embargo. Much to the annoyance of the inhabitants of the White House, Castro has almost survived nine US presidents, who have consistently underestimated the huge reservoirs of support that still remain for the revolution. Popular support, unlike in Eastern Europe and the former Soviet Union in the 1970s and 1980s, has sustained the Castro government in a period of extreme isolation.

Nevertheless, the Cuban regime and the Cuban economy has been driven back. Castro, obviously seeking to apply what he considers are the lessons of Lenin's New Economic Policy, opened up the economy to foreign investment and even to foreign ownership of sections of the economy. Circulation of US dollars was legalised, which in the long run poses a huge threat to the planned economy. Prior to 1991, 85% of Cuban exports went to the USSR and Eastern Europe. This market was cut and exports plunged by 70%. This, in turn, resulted in a one-third drop in the Cuban economy in 1991.

The effects of this collapse have still not been made up by the end of the 1990s and the beginning of the new century. Although there has been a certain recovery in the economy huge lay-offs of workers have taken place. The regime has taken measures to ensure that healthcare and education have been defended. Nevertheless, this has not been enough to prevent the return of some of the worst aspects of life under capitalism. The majority of industry is still concentrated in the hands of the state, but capitalism seeks a comeback through the pores of the black economy. According to the Financial Times,

"The vast majority of Cuba's 4.6 million workforce is employed by the state and still earn their basic salaries in pesos." [147]

There is a parallel economy based upon the 'greenback', the US dollar. Many Cubans cannot manage on the average monthly wage, which the Cuban government says rose to 223 pesos in 1999. There is also discontent about poor housing and transport. The Cuban government claims that the economy is growing by 6.2% and is an indication of a recovery. In one sense this is an indication:

"That the Cuban economy has weathered the worst of the severe recession that followed the collapse of the former Soviet bloc". [148]

It is clear that while US imperialism maintains its blockade there is a division amongst the contending imperialist powers, who are jockeying for a favourable position in Cuba. They are preparing for the situation when they expect that there will be a liquidation of the planned economy. Canada is now Cuba's leading trade and investment partner, followed by Spain. By 1996 there were an estimated 650 foreign companies with investments in Cuba. Other more powerful Latin American capitalist countries, such as Mexico and Brazil, have followed suit with a view to extending their economic and political influence in the region. This is done in order to gain advantages for themselves, but is also a means of pressurising the Cuban bureaucracy to take steps towards a restoration of capitalism and the winding-up of the planned economy.

With the model of what happened in Eastern Europe and the former Soviet Union in mind, they hope that the Cuban bureaucracy, or at least decisive sections of it, could transform itself into a capitalist class, together with a section of the Cuban exile population in Florida. However, this perspective is complicated because of the situation in the US. The ultra-right wing Cuban exiles in Miami wish to 'starve out' the Castro regime and, if possible, overthrow his government by force of arms. The Republicans, also, are not in favour of any 'compromise' with the Castro regime – although it is doubtful whether they now wish to maintain the US embargo of Cuba because this is to the disadvantage of US imperialism. Wall Street, in the main, certainly wants to end the blockade. It sees foreign companies buying up Cuban assets and now clearly recognises that 'engagement' with Cuba is the best way to speed up the end of the planned economy and the demise of Castro. The decision of the Clinton administration to face down the Cuban exiles and reunite the Cuban boy Elian Gonzalez with his father underlines the change in the attitude of the majority in the US and of the US ruling class towards Cuba. The whole episode represented a severe defeat for the Cuban exiles who hitherto have exercised an influence over both the Democrats and the Republicans out of proportion to their size or weight in the US population.

There is also a body of the exiles who would want to seek a compromise with Castro as a transition to the restoration of capitalism. But that section who are thirsting for revenge, look towards reclaiming their property in Cuba and instituting a bloody settling of accounts with Castro and his supporters. All of these factors, particularly the hatred of the role of US imperialism in Cuba and throughout Latin America, has ensured that the Cuban regime, and particularly Castro, has been able to retain support despite the enormous collapse in the 1990s. Nevertheless, the objective situation, if it continues for any length of time, will compel Cuba to implement more and more pro-capitalist pressures.

Castro, of course, presents this as a temporary policy and still proclaims his continued support for 'socialism'. Nevertheless, his manoeuvring with the different imperialist powers and figures shows the character of the Cuban regime. He has defended 'socialism' but, at the same time, has feted and welcomed the hated pro-Thatcherite former Spanish finance minister, Solchaga, who visited Havana as an economics adviser. Castro shamefully even declared his desire to meet Thatcher in person and has already met the Pope as part of a clear overture to the Catholic Church. At the same time, as Tony Saunois has pointed out, Castro has remained silent about the uprisings of the indigenous people in Chiapas, Mexico.[149]

Cuba faces a choice of two roads in the next period. The processes of capitalist restoration, could be accelerated, if anything, in the next period with the continuation of the present policies of the Castro government. This scenario could only be definitely averted through the establishment of a genuine regime of workers' democracy, linked to the perspective of carrying the idea of the socialist revolution to Latin America and internationally. Notwithstanding the blandishments of the DSP, this would involve the establishment of genuine workers' councils, locally and nationally, which would have control and management of the economy as a whole. All representatives and officials must be elected, subject to recall by those they represent and receive only the average wage of a skilled worker. In short, Cuba needs a regime of workers' democracy.

The one-party regime should be scrapped. As Tony Saunois points out:
"This is often justified because of the threat to the revolution from imperialism and the prospect of reactionary right-wing gangs from Miami being allowed to organise their forces. This threat is real but will not be averted by only allowing the party of the

bureaucracy to organise itself. All parties which are opposed to imperialism and defend the idea of a socialist planned economy should be allowed to organise, conduct propaganda and stand candidates in elections." [150]

Independent trade unions should be established separate from the state but in support of a planned economy and a democratic workers' state. Ultimately, the threat of capitalist restoration and the defeat of the Cuban Revolution can only be avoided through the international victory of the socialist revolution and, as a first step, its victory in Latin America. For this it is necessary to win the support of the working class in Latin America to establish a socialist federation of the continent. We believe that this programme is the only way of carrying forward the great achievements of the Cuban revolution. Cuba needs genuine Marxism, the programme of workers' democracy, in order to rekindle and regenerate all the best traditions that led to its victory more than four decades ago.

This cannot be provided by those like the DSP who have a one-sided view of the Cuban Revolution and the present situation in Cuba. The analysis, programme and perspectives of the Committee for a Workers' International offers the best hope of preserving the gains of the Cuban Revolution as well as helping to prepare for a new phase of victorious struggle of the workers and peasants of Latin America.

Appendix

This pamphlet was first published in three articles in Militant, on 27 January, 3 and 10 February, 1978. They were published together as a pamphlet, 'Cuba: Analysis of the Revolution'. Some minor alterations were made in order to render the analysis of the Cuban Revolution more precise.

THE CUBAN REVOLUTION

Events in Africa and the Caribbean have once again forced Cuba back onto the world stage. Having pressed South African forces to invade Angola in an attempt to defeat the revolution, US imperialism then foamed at the mouth when Cuban troops and material were used to support the MPLA. This probably turned the war in favour of the MPLA and resulted in the elimination of landlordism and capitalism in Angola.

At the same time, Cuba has become a pole of attraction for those countries of the Caribbean, like Jamaica and Guyana, which have been devastated by the world slump of 1974-75. To the masses of Latin America, moreover, in the vice of military dictatorships and plagued by hunger and famine – as in Argentina and Chile – Cuba seems to be a haven of progress and tranquillity.

In the advanced industrialised countries also the charismatic figures of the Cuban Revolution, like Fidel Castro and the murdered Che Guevara, contrast favourably in the eyes of some sections of youth looking to end capitalism as against the grey figures like Brezhnev and Kosygin. Even Arthur Scargill, when challenged by David Frost on a recent TV programme, gave Cuba as a model of the society he was aiming for.

Can Cuba act as a guide either for the workers and peasants of the backward countries or the labour movement in the advanced capitalist world in the struggle against capitalism? What is the nature of the Cuban regime? These questions can only be answered by examining the causes and subsequent development of the Cuban Revolution.

Before the revolution, Cuba was a paradise for the rich – a playground particularly for American tourists – but a nightmare for the workers and peasants. In 1950-54 the average per capita income in Delaware, the richest state in the United States of America, was $2,279, while in Cuba it was only $312, ie $6 a week. Even in Mississippi, the poorest state in the USA, average per capita income stood at $829! Fifty-four per cent of the rural population had no toilets at all – not even a privy, and malaria, tuberculosis and syphilis were rampant. There was 25 per cent illiteracy and a similar percentage were unemployed at any one time, ie one in four of the population. Fewer children proportionately of school age went to school in the 1950s than in the 1920s, yet Havana in 1954 had more Cadillacs than any other city in the world!

At the same time, the land was concentrated in a few hands, in huge latifundia. One hundred and fourteen farms, or fewer than 0.1 per cent of the total number, encompassed 20.1 per cent of the land. Eight per cent of the total number made up 71.1 per cent of the land while at the other end of the scale 39 per cent of the total number of farms were made up of small peasant holdings of less than one acre – but they encompassed only 3.3 per cent of the land.

Imperialism dominates

Moreover, the Cuban economy was dominated by the giant American monopolies. Thus the share of US firms was 90 per cent in the telephone and electric services, about 50 per cent in public services and 40 per cent in raw sugar. Bound with iron hoops to the American economy, Cuba was compelled to concentrate on one main crop, sugar, for the American market. Most of Cuba's sugar was exported to the US under a fixed yearly quota and set prices.

Crowning the whole system was the dictatorship of the gangster Batista. It was estimated that between his second seizure of power in 1953 and his overthrow in 1959, upwards of 20,000 died at the hands of his soldiers and torturers.

Cuba in the 1950s had not been able to carry through the tasks of the capitalist democratic revolution, ie land to the peasants, freedom from the stranglehold of foreign economic and political domination and the development of industry along modern lines. The experience of the Russian Revolution – brilliantly anticipated by Leon Trotsky's theory of the permanent revolution – demonstrated that only the working class in the backward countries is able to lead the nation in completing these tasks. Once having come to power and having carried through the capitalist democratic revolution, the working class of Russia went over to the socialist tasks – nationalisation of the commanding heights of the economy – and also provided the spark for the beginning of the international socialist revolution.

'Progressive'

Contrary to this experience and the methods of Lenin and the Bolsheviks, the Cuban Communist Party – in line with most of the Communist Parties of Latin America today – stood for an alliance with the so-called 'progressive national bourgeoisie' as the means of completing the 'anti-imperialist patriotic and democratic revolution'. But the Cuban capitalists invested in land and the owners of the big latifundia in industry. No serious land reform could be carried through with the support of the Cuban capitalists. Nor were they capable of leading a struggle against

US imperialism upon whom they leaned for defence against the Cuban masses. The hunt for the mythical 'progressive national capitalists' led the Cuban CP into actually supporting Batista soon after he first took power in 1933.

To begin with, party leader Blas Roca condemned Batista as "that national traitor in the pay of the imperialists". But in 1938 the CP Central Committee had discovered that Batista had "ceased to be the leading figure in the reactionary camp"! This magical transformation had been occasioned by the fact that Batista had been granted 'democratic' credentials by none other than US President Franklin Roosevelt. Moreover, the humble origins of 'Sergeant Batista' meant that he now received the benediction of the CP leaders. Batista reciprocated by legalising the CP in 1938 and four years later he took two CP ministers into his Cabinet! Blas Roca – who was later to sit in Castro's Cabinet – appeared on the same balcony as Batista in 1942 to receive the cheers of the Cuban masses. Notwithstanding their support, Batista was forced out of office in 1944. Fidel Castro, on the other hand, was denounced by the CP in 1947 as a "gangster"! Even later, when the CP was compelled to change its attitude towards Castro, they still doubted that Batista would be overthrown by the guerrillas, and in November 1958 called for a "democratic coalition government".

Batista's second coup in 1952 provoked widespread opposition in Cuba and particularly from the students and intellectuals, like Fidel Castro and his brother Raúl. With 120 followers they launched an attack on the Moncada barracks on 26 July, 1953. This was defeated, and Castro was first imprisoned and then released only to go to Mexico to organise a guerrilla force which landed in Cuba in 1956. In a heroic three-year struggle they launched a guerrilla campaign which, with the support of the impoverished peasantry, resulted in the defeat of the overwhelmingly numerically superior Batista's force. Some of Batista's soldiers and even officers were won over to the side of the guerrillas.

Harmony

In 1961, faced with a life and death struggle with American imperialism, Castro was to claim that "he had always been a Marxist-Leninist at heart". At the same time, as KS Karol ironically remarks in his book Guerrillas in Power:

"Some of his comrades who were even less entitled to that label, claimed they had all the time been Marxists without knowing it while others had never been anti-Communist and were therefore open to conversion".

The truth is that Castro, up to this stage, had been no more than a radical middle-class democrat whose ideal was democratic capitalist America. Thus, to the American journalist Herbert Matthews, in an interview during the struggle against Batista, he declared:

"You can be sure we have no animosity towards the United States and the American people... we are fighting for a democratic Cuba and an end to dictatorship." [New York Times, 24 February, 1957]

Moreover, in a document of Castro's movement – the 26 July Movement – in 1956, it stated that it adhered to "Jeffersonian philosophy" and subscribed to the *"Lincoln formula"*, and proclaimed the desire *"to reach a state of solidarity and harmony between capital and labour in order to raise productivity"*.

Even after he had ousted Batista, Castro declared on 6 March, 1959, to the Association of Bankers, that he desired their collaboration. He also added, according to the US 'News and World Report', that he had "no intention of nationalising any industries". Perhaps this was a 'crafty ruse' merely meant to fool the landlords and capitalists? On the contrary, all the evidence shows that Castro and his supporters never started off their struggle with a clear socialist programme and perspectives as had Lenin and the Bolsheviks in Russia.

Lenin based himself on the working class. He anticipated that the workers would lead the poor peasantry in a struggle against Tsarism. Castro and Guevara relied on the peasants and the rural population. The working class only entered the struggle through a general strike in Havana when the guerrillas had already triumphed and Batista was fleeing for his life. The dominant role of the Russian working class with the conscious management and control of the state and industry which they exercised through workers' and peasants' councils – the most democratic institutions ever seen – led to a powerful movement of the working class of the world rallying to the cause of their Russian brothers. They attempted to emulate the Russian Revolution in their own countries.

Impasse

The fact that Castro came to power through a predominantly rural movement shaped the whole character of his movement. It was only a peculiar combination of circumstances which resulted in Castro – who to begin with never envisaged going beyond the framework of a capitalist democracy – presiding over the expropriation of the landlords and capitalists.

On the one side, was the utter bankruptcy of Cuban capitalism to show a way out of the impasse of society. At the same time, there was the colossal pressure of an aroused peasantry and the working class. With the defeat of Batista, the peasants moved to occupy the land and the working class clamoured for wage increases and the reinstatement of those sacked under the previous regime. Thus, in the spring of 1959, 6,000 workers of the Cuban Electric Company declared a slowdown in order to achieve a 20 per cent rise in wages, and 600 workers who had been dismissed in 1957-58 began a strike before the presidential palace. The masses were armed and formed into the militia. Meanwhile, the representative of American imperialism,

Eisenhower, panic-stricken by the radicalisation of the Cuban masses, sought to pressurise and blackmail the Cuban government into submission.

Resistance

This came to a head over Russian crude oil which was to be delivered to Cuba under a trade agreement between the two countries signed in January, 1960. In June the three big oil companies (Jersey Standard, Texaco and Shell), under pressure from the US government, refused to refine the Russian oil. But the Cuban government then 'intervened' (a form of supervision) and put the oil through. The companies retaliated by refusing to deliver oil from Venezuela. Cuba then agreed to take all its oil from Russia.

The Eisenhower administration hit back in July by cutting the remaining 700,000 tons of Cuban sugar due to be delivered under the quota agreement. This was calculated to bring the Castro regime to its knees. But Russia immediately stepped in and agreed to take the 700,000 tons of sugar. At the same time, on 6 August, the Cuban Telephone Company, the Electric Company, the oil refinery and all the sugar mills – which up to then had only been 'intervened' – were all nationalised. In the next four months, in a rapid succession of blows and counter-blows, all Cuban and American big business was taken over.

In September, the Cuban subsidiaries of United States' companies were taken over. Cuban companies were taken over in October and by the end of 1960 capitalism had been eliminated in Cuba. US imperialism retaliated by declaring a complete trade embargo and preparing for a military intervention to crush the Cuban Revolution.

The pressure of the masses, the weakness of Cuban capitalism, and the miscalculations and blunders of American imperialism, all combined to push the Castro regime into expropriating landlordism and capitalism. We thus witnessed in Cuba a verification of Trotsky's theory of the permanent revolution in a caricatured form. The capitalist democratic revolution could only be carried out against the resistance of the capitalists in Cuba and internationally. This, in turn, compelled Castro to lean on the masses and to go over to nationalise big business and establish a planned economy. There was no conscious foresight nor a worked-out perspective, as with Lenin and Trotsky in the Russian Revolution. Indeed, if Castro could have been shown before the revolution a film of his subsequent development he probably would have condemned it as a monstrous fabrication!

The Soviets, with democratic control and management of the state, together with the consciousness on the part of the masses that the fate of the revolution was bound up with the victory of the world revolution, were decisive in provoking the revolutionary movement of the working class in Europe and the world following the Russian Revolution. Because they could see their own class in power, despite the monstrous slanders of their rulers, the workers of Europe and the world came to the assistance and tried to emulate their Russian brothers in the stormy events of 1918 and 1919.

Earthquake

The Cuban Revolution had the effect of an earthquake – particularly in Latin America. But because of the forces involved – a predominantly peasant army – and the absence of conscious control and management by the working class and poor peasants, the Cuban Revolution could not have the same effect as the Russian Revolution. A workers' state had been established – almost in the jaws of American imperialism – but a deformed workers' state, with power concentrated in the hands of a layer of privileged officials.

POWER IN THE HANDS OF A BUREAUCRATIC ELITE

The elimination of landlordism and capitalism in Cuba in 1960 sent shock waves throughout North and South America. Determined to snuff out the revolution at the earliest opportunity US imperialism financed and armed the invasion force which landed in Cuba at Playa Girón (Bay of Pigs) in April 1961.

The invaders masqueraded as the 'saviours' of the Cuban Revolution. The fact that 1,500 men of the invasion force had once owned between them a million acres of land, 10,000 houses, 70 factories, five mines, two banks and ten sugar mills was, of course, purely coincidental!

But the mass basis of the revolution ensured the defeat of this and other counter-revolutionary attempts of the CIA-backed émigrés. Without doubt the Castro regime enjoyed enormous popular support.

The masses were armed in the 200,000 strong workers' and peasants' militia. The conservative historian of the Cuban Revolution, Hugh Thomas, recorded the comments of a fifteen-year old armed schoolboy in 1961:

"We Cubans are an army people." [Thomas, p1321]

There was undoubtedly an element of workers' control in the factories in the first period of the revolution and every neighbourhood and street had a 'Committee for the Defence of the Revolution'.

An indication of the widespread support for the regime is demonstrated by the enormous crowds which gathered in Havana to listen to Castro's speeches. At the meeting where Castro delivered what came to be known as the 'Second Declaration of Havana', one million – out of a total of six million – gathered in Plaza de la Revolución on 4 February, 1962!

But at the same time the masses had no control or management of the state machine. KS Karol, in his book Guerrillas in Power – which is mostly sympathetic to Castro and the Cuban Revolution – comments on his visit to Cuba in 1961:

"These enthusiastic people [the working class and the poor peasants] would have had to talk about their 'soviets' or about their 'socialist plans' (for the revolution to be comparable to Russia or the Spanish Civil War). Now I had tried in vain, in the provinces as well as in Havana, to find signs of any great enthusiasm for either among the rank and file. There was an impressive amount of support for the revolution but the absence of political initiative even among the militia and the rather primitive level of socialism was rather surprising". [Karol, pp39-40]

The plebiscitary nature of the state – which is a feature of Bonapartism – was shown in the mass meetings addressed by Castro. The workers were called upon to say "Sí" or "No", but not to discuss or decide on issues.

Hungarian Revolution

But without the conscious control and management by the masses themselves, the development of a new elite is inevitable. Even in Russia with brilliant leaders like Lenin and Trotsky and the conscious participation of the working class in the running of society, bureaucratic degeneration was inevitable so long as the revolution was isolated in a backward country.

The Bolsheviks envisaged that the Russian Revolution would provoke the revolution in Europe, which would then come to the assistance of Russia with economic aid, technicians etc. The beginning of socialism and with it the dissolution of the state machine is only possible on the basis of a level of production higher than the highest level of production reached by capitalism, ie higher than capitalist America.

A Socialist United States of Europe leading to a Socialist World Federation would undoubtedly have enabled this to be realised. But the isolation of the revolution to a single country – and a backward country at that – led to the bureaucratic degeneration of Russia personified by the rise of Stalin. The masses were elbowed aside by the bureaucratic elite from any real say in the running of the country.

But in Cuba, right from the outset, management and control was concentrated in the hands of Castro and his supporters, the officialdom in the state machine, the governing party and the army, etc.

The character of the regime was demonstrated by the contrasting attitude adopted by the Russian bureaucracy towards the Cuban Revolution on the one hand and the Hungarian Revolution on the other. The existence of Soviets in Hungary in 1956, with power in the hands of the masses, was a mortal threat to the bureaucratic upstarts. If it was allowed to succeed similar uprisings – political revolutions – would have swept through Eastern Europe and Russia itself. The bureaucracy could not compromise with the Hungarian Revolution. The 'liberal' Khrushchev determined to drown the revolution in blood.

Towards the Castro regime, however, the Russian bureaucracy extended the hand of friendship. Indeed, without massive Russian aid – in excess of $1 million a day – the Cuban Revolution would have collapsed. Forty per cent of Cuba's foreign trade is with Russia. Ninety-five per cent of its oil comes from the same source while the Russian bureaucracy is to pay 30 cents a pound for Cuban sugar – compared to 14 cents a pound when the agreement was signed in 1975 – under the agreement which is to last until 1980. Moreover, the enormous estimated debt of between $3 billion and $4 billion owed to Russia was deferred under the same scheme.

"He who pays the piper calls the tune". During one quarrel with the Cuban regime a Russian embassy official is reputed to have arrogantly declared: "We have only to say that repairs are being held up in Baku for three weeks and that's that"!

Differences there have undoubtedly been between Castro and the Russian bureaucracy – involving also its acolytes in the 'Communist' Parties of Latin America – but the Cuban Revolution posed no real threat to the privileged elite in Russia. On the contrary, the establishment of a regime basically similar to its own on the doorstep of American imperialism served to strengthen the power and the prestige of the Russian bureaucracy.

Planned Economy

Yet the enormous aid extended together with the advantages which flow from a planned economy has meant a gigantic development of Cuban society – particularly when compared to the unemployment, the starvation, and the misery which stalks the Latin American continent. In practically every field the living standards of the Cuban masses have outdistanced those of their Latin American counterparts. Thus, by 1975, the infant mortality rate – 27.4 per thousand – was the lowest in the whole of Latin America.

The life expectancy in Cuba is now 69.2 years compared to 45.3 years in Bolivia, 58.5 in Colombia, 59.7 in Brazil and 60.6 in Chile. Before 1959, half the children of primary school age had no education at all.

Today, all receive some education and there are now almost two million primary school pupils compared to less than 720,000 before 1959, and 79,000 primary school teachers now compared to 17,000 then. Day nurseries are available to all children from the 45th day. Even historian Hugh Thomas conceded:

"Few die of malnutrition and, in the country, particularly in Oriente province, the very poor peasants must be fed better than before the revolution... unemployment has undoubtedly fallen despite the new use in the economy of many once housebound women." [Thomas, p1425]

Contrast this to Argentina where it is estimated that living standards have dropped by 50 per cent since the army took power!

Moreover, from an unlikely source, Mr Pat Holt, the Secretary to the US Senate

Foreign Relations Committee, in June 1974, came confirmation of the remarkable development of Cuba since the revolution: "The island in 1973 has the highest per capita income in Latin America ($1,578) with the exception of Venezuela." And Venezuela is only ahead of Cuba because of its rich oil resources.

On the other hand, Cuba remains a predominantly agricultural country with sugar still the main product. In 1974, 85 per cent of foreign exchange earnings came from sugar. But at the same time there has been a development of industry. Thus, between 1959 and 1965, industrial production increased by 50 per cent. In 1975, the economy increased by something like 9 per cent. Nickel has now surpassed tobacco as the country's second most valuable export after sugar. Steel production is planned to increase in the next period to about one million tons. As striking as these achievements are, they are as nothing compared to what could have been achieved on the basis of workers' democracy.

Mismanagement, tremendous waste and zigzags in economic policy are inevitable without the planning, checking, control and initiative which is only possible through workers' democracy. This is as necessary to a planned economy as is oxygen to a body. Without it the pores clog up and virtual seizure of the organism is inevitable at a certain stage.

This is now the situation in Russia and Eastern Europe where the bureaucratic caste of Brezhnev and Co are now an absolute fetter on the further development of society. In an undeveloped country like Cuba the bureaucracy can still play a relatively progressive role in developing industry – by borrowing the technique of the advanced countries and seeking to catch up with them – but at the cost of colossal overheads. Mismanagement and waste has been evident from the first days of the Cuban Revolution.

Thus, in 1963, in the first flush of enthusiasm Castro accepted Khrushchev's offer of 1,000 tractors to mechanise the sugar harvest. But only after they had arrived in Cuba was it discovered that they were unsuitable for cutting sugar cane which requires special machines! At the same time Che Guevara – in a secret speech which was for the *"private use of political and economic leaders"* [Karol, Guerrillas in Power] – castigated managers for poor quality of goods.

He pointed out that:

"There is at present a shortage of toothpaste… Only when the reserves began to run out and no raw materials were coming in, did those responsible become galvanised into action… undeterred the comrades succeeded in making a toothpaste pleasing to the eye and as clean and white as any, but which hardens after a while… in a few months' time people are going to object because we are selling them stones in tubes"!

From the top

Guevara and Castro bemoaned the symptoms but were unable either to diagnose the disease or prescribe the cure. Arbitrary decision and low quality goods which accompany them are inevitable in a regime where the 'decision makers' are not subject to mass criticism, election and recall. So also are the crises and the zigzags in economic policy, which have characterised the Castro regime from the beginning.

Thus, in 1961, Guevara predicted that Cuba would be an industrialised country within 12 months! Given the weaknesses of the Cuban economy such a perspective was utterly utopian – even with the enormous assistance of the Russian bureaucracy. Shortly afterwards this gave way to a concentration on agriculture and particularly on sugar. But the targets on sugar production were decided by the tops and handed down to the masses.

The real possibilities in a planned economy can only be decided on the basis of thoroughgoing discussion among the masses who can add the necessary correctives, additions, etc. Without this discussion and a reliance on mass initiative to implement the plans, blunders and mistakes are inevitable.

This has proved to be the case in Cuba in relation to the sugar industry. Thus, Castro declared that Cuba would produce 10 million tons of sugar by 1970. Yet, even given the vagaries of the weather – where agriculture is concerned – it was subsequently demonstrated that such a target would only have been possible on the basis of the mechanisation and development of industry. Only this would allow the harmonious development of industry and agriculture together. Leon Trotsky showed in his criticisms of Stalin's blunder on agriculture that a correct correlation between industry and agriculture is impossible on the basis of a regime of bureaucratic absolutism.

Without committing the same crimes as Stalin, Castro nevertheless attempted to substitute the massive use of voluntary and sometimes forced labour for Cuba's lack of the industrial and technical means of realising the targets which had been set. Thus, in the drive for the 10 million tons of sugar, over 400,000 Cubans were mobilised in the harvest of 1970. Industrial workers, housewives and the youth were mobilised to bring in the harvest at the cost of an enormous disruption and dislocation of industry. Yet only 8.5 million tons of sugar was produced. In 1975, only 5.4 million tons were harvested and even by 1980 it is now planned to produce 8.7 million tons; a clear demonstration of the sheer impracticability on the basis of the present regime of the earlier targets.

Preceding this, the regime launched the 'Great Revolutionary Offensive' – a Cuban version of the 'Cultural Revolution'. Denunciations of 'bureaucracy' and the virtual militarisation of labour, was combined with the proclamations about 'moving towards Communism' and a campaign to eliminate small businesses. In 1968, something like 58,000 small businesses – including shops, stalls and even 9,179 craftsmen working on their own – were nationalised!

The government then claimed that Cuba was now the "socialist country with the largest nationalised sector". But to eliminate every small business without first of all creating the conditions whereby the state trusts are in a position to supply the goods – particularly the consumer goods – and services provided by these firms added enormously to the general scarcity of certain goods which in turn led to growing discontent. The purpose of the campaign was also to cut down the privileges of the bureaucracy to accumulate the necessary resources for industrialisation and the mechanisation of agriculture and in a forced march to reach the targets, which had been arbitrarily decided by the government.

Similar boasts in relation to living standards were also made by Castro. Thus, in 1960, he predicted that Cuba would enjoy a living standard comparable to Sweden by 1965. The next year severe rationing of food and clothes was introduced! Rationing continued right up to the 1970s and has only been eased or ended in some consumer goods in the last few years.

FOR A SOCIALIST UNITED STATES OF THE CARIBBEAN AND LATIN AMERICA

Faced with an impasse Castro was forced to alter course. Thus, in November 1973 at the 'Congress of Trade Unions', he admitted that, *"Cuba was not ready for communism and must in some certain respects go backwards due to the revolutionary inexperience of many Cubans and the low rate of production in some sectors of the economy."*

On 14 January, 1974, he also confessed that *"more workers were required to carry out the same jobs than had been the case under American ownership".*

Only four hours of productive work per day was the national average in Cuba in 1966. Absenteeism had reached 16 per cent in light industry and 31 per cent in the food industry. Castro declared in 1975: *"The people can replace anyone; me as well if they want,"* and called for more participation in decision making.

In reality there were no democratic channels for the masses to change the policies or their leaders. Thus, KS Karol remarks:

"All its [the Communist Party's] organs from the Central Committee down to the lowest office are appointed from the top by Fidel Castro and his closest collaborators." [Karol, Guerrillas in Power, p458]

The Castroite Cuban CP was established in 1965 yet its first Congress was held in 1975! Even during the Russian Civil War under the leadership of Lenin and Trotsky the Bolshevik Party held its conference every year.

It was left to Dr Jorge Risquest, Castro's Minister of Labour, to give an inkling of the real causes of this malaise. In July 1975, he attributed *"the country's economic problems mainly to a widespread passive resistance by the workers"*. He also admitted that *"there was no proper rapport between workers on the one hand and the state administration, the officials of the Communist Party and the trade unions on the other"*.

As a means of ventilating the accumulated grievances against the bureaucracy a draft constitution was published in 1975 establishing so-called 'popular power'. Experimental elections were held for 'municipal assemblies' in the Matanzas province in the same year. Usually two candidates stood but sometimes as many as 15 participated in the election.

One Party

But the rub was that all candidates had to be members of the Communist Party, or constituent organisations of this party, like the Young Communist League! In other words, the elections were a farce. Imagine the reaction of the British workers if they were told they could support candidates from only one party in shop stewards' or trade union elections!

The apologists of the Castroite regime – some of them alleged 'Trotskyists' – object that Castro has not hesitated to denounce bureaucracy and the Russian bureaucracy in particular – characterising them as 'pseudo-revolutionaries' – in the past. Moreover, they say Castro attempted to spread the revolution to the Latin American mainland, thereby coming into conflict with Communist Party leaders in the area.

Stalin, Mao Zedong and Tito have all in their time denounced the 'bureaucracy'. But they attacked the excesses of their own system, making scapegoats of the most glaring and blatant cases of bureaucratic mismanagement, waste and greed, the better to defend as a whole the privileges of the caste that they represented. Castro clashed with the Russian bureaucracy when the interests of the Cuban state were threatened. Thus, in 1962 and later in 1968, he denounced Aníbal Escalante as an arch-bureaucrat.

But behind the conflict with Escalante was the clash between two national bureaucracies. Escalante – a leader of the Cuban CP before it fused with the Castroites – was a pliable tool of the Russian bureaucracy, echoing their behind-the-scenes criticisms of Castro, denouncing his 'ungratefulness' to his Russian benefactors, and his 'adventurism' on the Latin American mainland. Yet the manner of dealing with him spoke as much against the methods of Castro as Escalante.

Guerrilla War

Escalante was accused of organising a 'micro-faction', a crime which did not even exist under Cuban law! Compare the attitude of Castro to that of Lenin at the time of the Russian Civil War. Lenin conceded the right of Bukharin, Radek and others to publish a daily paper which passionately argued against Lenin's views on the Brest-

Litovsk Peace Treaty and other related issues!

To be sure, in the first period when the lava of revolution had not cooled down we witnessed the Second Declaration of Havana with its brilliant denunciation of the misery of the Latin American masses and the call to revolution. Che Guevara was murdered in a heroic but futile guerrilla adventure in Bolivia. But Castro denounced the opportunist Communist Parties – particularly in Venezuela – not for its abandonment of revolutionary perspectives but its refusal to take to arms and embrace his guerrillaist strategy.

At no time did Castro look towards the powerful working class of Latin America as the main agency for socialist change. Artificially attempting to transfer the guerrilla experience of the Cuban Revolution to the Latin American mainland all hope was placed on the peasantry. The reason for this attempt to extend the experience of the Cuban Revolution to Latin America was to be found in the vicious trade embargo against Cuba enforced by American imperialism and its satellites in the continent.

But foreign policy is a continuation of home policy. The consolidation of the Cuban bureaucracy together with the easing of the boycott was bound to result in a change in the foreign policy of the regime with attempts to find an accommodation with US imperialism and its cohorts in Latin America to the detriment of even verbal support for revolution in the continent.

Thus, when the veiled military dictatorship in Mexico massacred more than 300 students in October 1968 not a word of protest was forthcoming from the Cuban government or Communist Party. The students had proclaimed their support of the Cuban regime but Mexico was one of the few capitalist governments to have maintained diplomatic relations with Cuba! The national interests of the Cuban state took precedence over 'international solidarity'.

Similarly, there was stony silence in Havana when 10 million workers in France occupied the factories and shook capitalism in Europe and the world to its foundations. Not even a message of support for their French counterparts emanated from the state-controlled student movement, the UJC-FEU!

This tendency will inevitably be reinforced with the lifting of US imperialism's boycott of Cuba and the establishment of diplomatic relations between the two countries. The Carter Administration is prepared to recognise the Cuban regime once it abandons its intervention in the African continent. With undisguised satisfaction US imperialism recognises that the Castro regime has abandoned its earlier 'adventures' in Latin America.

Privileges

Disillusionment with Castro also began to set in among his most fervent Latin American supporters. In 1967, Castro denounced the Venezuelan Communist Party and supported the guerrilla struggle of Douglas Bravo. But by 1970:

"According to Bravo, the Castroites stopped aiding the Latin American revolution the moment they decided to concentrate on their own economic problems and to rally to the Soviet Union." [Karol, Guerrillas in Power, p536]

Castro underlined the nature of his regime with his support for the intervention of the Russian bureaucracy in Czechoslovakia in 1968. Shortly afterwards, one of his ministers, Llanusa, told students in 1968: *"We shall not have a Czechoslovakia here."* These developments are not at all some kind of an aberration. Ideas don't drop from the sky. In the mouths of political leaders they reflect the material interests of classes or social groupings in society.

The Cuban bureaucracy now fears both the victory of the socialist revolution in the West and the political revolution against the bureaucracy in the East. Either would mean the replacement of this bureaucratic elite by workers' and peasants' democracy and the elimination of its privileges. Castro is the representative and supreme arbiter of the Cuban bureaucracy. Both in relation to the mighty events in France and in Czechoslovakia his attitude was a gauge of the fear which gripped the growing Cuban elite at these developments.

The elements of workers' control, the workers' militia, etc, which existed in the first period of the revolution have been either weakened or eliminated altogether. Thus, KS Karol writes:

"Cubans no longer boast about their workers' militia or about their Committees for Defence of the Revolution. The latter now have a purely repressive function."

The privileges of this layer have existed from the outset of the Cuban Revolution. But on a low economic and cultural base the differences between the workers and peasants on the one hand and the bureaucracy on the other could not be as great as in Russia or Eastern Europe. Nevertheless, even as early as 1963, KS Karol remarks that, in one factory he came across, an engineer received 17 times the wage of a worker!

Moreover, he cites other perks and privileges cornered by the bureaucracy, such as the "high class" restaurants, like 'Monsenor', the 'Torre', the '1830', the 'Floridita' and others which charge colossal prices for meals. At the CP Party Conference in 1975 a decision was taken to allow Cubans to buy cars --which up till then had been the preserve of the party and state officials!

With the development of the Cuban economy these differences, rather than disappearing, will grow apace. But with the differentiation of Cuban society so also will grow the opposition to the stifling atmosphere created by the ruling privileged stratum of officials.

From a relatively liberal atmosphere in the first period, suppression of all dissent has become the norm. Thus, in 1962, the works of Leon Trotsky were on sale in Havana and there was a flowering of culture and art. Now the dead hand of the bureaucracy pervades everything. Thus, unorthodox writers, poets and artists like Padilla are now frowned upon by the regime. As in Russia, China and Eastern Europe, the toleration of freedom for artists threatens to provoke a movement of the masses for the same rights. The Hungarian Revolution began with the writers' opposition gathered together in the Petofi Circle.

The Cuban Revolution has demonstrated the gigantic possibilities which flow from nationalisation and a plan of production. In the statistics which record the rise in health care, education, social security and the development of the economy, it has been more than justified. It has also given a big push to the revolution in the Caribbean and in Latin America.

But because the revolution took place in a backward country with a leadership which based itself on a predominantly agrarian movement and with national limitations, bureaucratic degeneration was inevitable. Undoubtedly the Castro regime still has much more of a popular base than the Stalinist regimes in Russia and Eastern Europe. But the development of industry will also mean the growth of the working class and with it increasing demands for workers' democracy. Moreover, political revolution in Eastern Europe or the social revolution in Europe, America or Japan will have their repercussions in Cuba itself.

The victory of the socialist revolution in Argentina or Brazil, for instance, would have a dramatic effect on Cuba. In these countries the social weight of the working class is so decisive that the socialist revolution would develop along the lines of the Russian Revolution. A victory of the working class in either country would detonate the socialist revolution throughout the continent and lead to a new revolution in Cuba – this time a political revolution and the establishment of workers' democracy.

Like iron filings being pulled into a magnet the countries of Central, South and also even North America, together with the Caribbean, would be drawn into a great Socialist Federation of North and South America. The Cuban Revolution has shown the tremendous possibilities lodged within a planned economy. But even these achievements will pale beside the great possibilities which will open up on the basis of workers' democracy and a Socialist Federation. The Cuban Revolution demonstrates that only the socialist revolution and workers' democracy offers any salvation for the workers and peasants of Latin America and the Caribbean from the nightmare of landlordism and capitalism.

References

Cuba Today

1. Financial Times, London, 24 March, 1999
2. Keesing's Record of World Events, 1991, p37814
3. Ibid, p38141
4. The Independent, London, 20 July, 1998
5. Cuban Foreign Trade Minister, Ricardo Cabrisas, 2 May 1996, quoted in Keesing's, May 1996
6. The Guardian, London, 16 November, 1999
7. The Independent, 19 October, 1999
8. The Guardian, 10 August, 1998
9. John Percy, "A History of the Democratic Socialist Party – The First Two Decades", p33
10. Ibid, p35
11. Ibid, p47
12. This individual attended the International Executive Committee of the CWI in November 1997, as a visitor with full rights to speak and participate in the weeklong meeting. Yet, he achieved the rare feat of not uttering a word in the official discussions, and very little in any private discussions which took place!
13. Doug Lorimer, "The Cuban Revolution and Its Leadership: A Criticism of Peter Taaffe's Pamphlet 'Cuba: Analysis of the Revolution" in The Activist, p3
14. Percy, p37
15. Three Conceptions of the Russian Revolution, Writings of Leon Trotsky (1939-40), p59
16. Ibid, p60
17. Trotsky, The Permanent Revolution, Pathfinder, 1969, p142
18. Lorimer, "Trotsky's theory of Permanent Revolution: A Leninist critique" p13

19. Ibid, p14

20. Trotsky, The Permanent Revolution, pp171-2

21. Ibid, p226

22. Lorimer, The Cuban Revolution, p8

23. For example, John Bulaitis and Phil Hearse opposed our proposals to change the name of our party from Militant Labour to the Socialist Party. However, once our conference had rejected their position by a massive majority they promptly deserted, Hearse to Mexico City and Bulaitis to his own tiny sectarian organisation in Britain. Bulaitis has ended up as a self-confessed 'liquidationist'; he no longer believes in the need for a revolution-ary party based on the ideas of democratic centralism, while Hearse occasionally threatens to come out of retirement to denounce the CWI. He was invited to the DSP-sponsored 'Socialism 2000' held in Sydney at the beginning of that year.

24. Lorimer, The Cuban Revolution, p3

25. Ibid, p3

Lenin & Castro

26. Lorimer, The Cuban Revolution, p5

27. Peter Taaffe "Cuba: Analysis of the Revolution", p5

28. Lorimer, The Cuban Revolution, pp6-7

29. Carlos Franqui, Family Portrait with Fidel, p149

30. Ibid, pp152-153

31. Franqui, 'Journal de la révolution cubaine', quoted by Janette Habel, Cuba: the Revolution in Peril, p107

32. Franqui, Family Portrait with Fidel, p153

33. Ibid, pp153-154

34. Castro quoted in Hugh Thomas, 'Cuba – The Pursuit of Freedom', p829

35. Ibid, p831-2

36. Ibid, p833

37. Ibid, p921

38. Ibid, p921

39. Che Guevara, Notes for the Study of the Ideology of the Cuban Revolution, republished in Che Guevara and the Cuban Revolution, p133

40. Jon Lee Anderson, "Che Guevara: A Revolutionary Life", p235

41. Ibid, p245
42. Tad Szulc, "Fidel a Critical Portrait", p373
43. Ibid, p391
44. Lorimer, The Cuban Revolution, p7
45. John Reed, Ten Days That Shook the World, p129
46. Lorimer, The Cuban Revolution, p7
47. Che Guevara, The Essence of Guerrilla Struggle, the first part of chapter 1 of La guerra de guerrillas, republished in Che Guevara and the Cuban Revolution, pp76 and 77.
48. Thomas, pp1108-1109
49. Che Guevara and the Cuban Revolution, p79
50. Taaffe, p5

The World Balance of Forces

51. Szulc, pp397-398
52. Anderson p413
53. Ibid, p414
54. Ibid, p415
55. Szulc, p424
56. Andrew St George, 'A Visit with a Revolutionary', published in 'Coronet', February 1958, and reprinted in Robert Scheer and Maurice Zeitlin, 'Cuba: an American Tragedy', p63
57. Quoted by Scheer and Zeitlin, p64
58. Look magazine, November 1960, quoted by Scheer and Zeitlin, p64
59. Anderson, p476
60. Javier Pazoz, a son of a former president of the Cuban National Bank, who himself was a civil servant in the Ministry of Economics before going into exile, reported in New Republic, 12 January 1963 and quoted by Scheer and Zeitlin, p87
61. Anderson, p482
62. Ibid, p471
63. This is a reference to the Cuban Stalinists and not to genuine 'communists'.
64. Franqui, Family Portrait with Fidel, pp32-33
65. Interview in Scheer and Zeitlin, pp341-342
66. Franqui, Family Portrait with Fidel, pp76-77

67. Franqui is wrong to describe Russia as imperialist. It is true that the Russian bureaucracy acted in the world arena to ensure the maintenance and enhancement of their own national interests. However, it generally supplied Cuba and other states in the neo-colonial world with resources, particularly primary products, at below their prices on the world market.
68. Franqui, Family Portrait with Fidel pp77-78
69. Ibid, pp78-79
70. Ibid, pp104-105
71. Ibid, pp219-221
72. Szulc, pp428-429
73. Lorimer, The Cuban Revolution, p12
74. Ibid, p18
75. Szulc, p482
76. Ibid, p513
77. Ibid, p514
78. Ibid, p514
79. Ibid, p530
80. Ibid, p531
81. Ibid, p532
82. Ibid, pp532-533

Is there a Privileged Elite?
83. Lorimer, The Cuban Revolution, p13
84. Anderson, p593
85. Ibid p503
86. Maspero in Habel, preface, p.xxiii
87. Ibid, p.xxii
88. Aspillaga was associated with the British secret services.
89. Habel, pp58-60
90. Ibid, p60
91. Franqui, Family Portrait with Fidel, p145
92. Originally in Nation magazine by Maurice Zeitlin, republished in Scheer and Zeitlin, p238
93. Ibid, pp233-234
94. Ibid, p234

95. Ibid, p238
96. Ibid, p238
97. Zeitlin, "Cuba's Workers, Workers' Cuba, p.xvi
98. Ibid, pp xix-xx
99. Franqui, Family Portrait with Fidel, pp117-118
100. Ibid, p118
101. Zeitlin, 1969, pp.xxv-xxvi
102. Ibid, p.xxvii
103. Ibid, p.xxviii
104. Ibid, p.xxix
105. Ibid, p.xl
106. Ibid, p.xlvii (Zeitlin's emphasis)
107. Ibid, p.xlviii
108. KS Karol, Guerrillas in Power, pp184-185
109. Ibid, p328
110. Ibid, p452
111. Ibid, p459
112. Lorimer, The Cuban Revolution, p16
113. Habel, p81
114. Ibid, p81
115. Ibid, p82
116. Pisani, writing in Le Monde diplomatique, December 1987, quoted by Habel, p84
117. Szulc, p29
118. Ibid, p498
119. Félix de la Uz, quoted in Habel, p80
120. Pisani, ibid, quoted by Habel pp84-85
121. Habel, p85
122. Anderson, p416

Foreign Policy

123. Che Guevara, 'Cuba: Historical Exception or Vanguard of the Anti-Colonialist Struggle?' First published in Verde Olivio, 9 April, 1961, quoted in Anderson, p505
124. KS Karol, 'Cuba and the USSR', in 'Cuban Communism', p759

125. Marx was referring to the prolonged mass uprising of the peasants against feudalism in Germany in the sixteenth century.
126. The size and influence of the Indonesian working class is indicated by the following extract from the excellent pamphlet of the CWI on Indonesia: "The total labour force in Indonesia is 86 million strong. About 15% work in the manufacturing and petrochemical sector, 35% in service industries and 50% in agriculture. The number of industrial workers has vastly increased in recent decades because of the industrialisation of Indonesia. At the beginning of the '90s there was a big rise in the number of working class struggles. In 1994 there was a total of 1,130 strikes – an increase of 350% in relation to 1993! In the same year there were 100 student demonstrations and 50 peasant actions." ['Indonesia: An Unfinished Revolution']
127. Lorimer, The Cuban Revolution, p22
128. Ibid, pp22-23
129. Ibid, p23
130. Habel, p124
131. Lorimer, The Cuban Revolution, p24
132. Ibid, p26
133. Castro, speaking on 23 August 1968, quoted ibid, p24
134. Ibid, p26
135. Anderson, p586
136. Taaffe, p13
137. Lorimer, The Cuban Revolution, p26
138. Ibid, p27
139. Szulc, p527
140. Tony Saunois, Che Guevara, Symbol of Struggle, p54
141. Lorimer, The Cuban Revolution, p27
142. Szulc, p535

Conclusion
143. Szulc, p499
144. Ibid, pp499-500
145. Quoted in Szulc, p500
146. Ibid, pp498-499
147. Financial Times,4 January 2000
148. Ibid
149. Saunois, p62
150. Ibid, p63

Bibliography

Elie Abel, *The Missiles of October: The Cuban Missile Crisis 1962*, Mayflower-Dell, London, 1966

Jon Lee Anderson, *Che Guevara: A Revolutionary Life*, Bantam Press, 1997

Fidel Castro, *"Our line is the line of consistent anti-imperialism"*, a speech, Fair Play for Cuba Committee, Toronto, Canada, 1963

CWI, *Indonesia: An Unfinished Revolution*, 1998

Carlos Franqui, *Family Portrait with Fidel*, Jonathan Cape, 1983

Che Guevara, *Che Guevara and the Cuban Revolution*, Pathfinder/Pacific and Asia, Sydney, 1987

Che Guevara, *The Motorcycle Diaries: A Journey Around South America*, Fourth Estate, London, 1996 edition

Janette Habel, *Cuba: the Revolution in Peril*, Verso 1991

Marta Harnecker, *Cuba: Dictatorship or Democracy*, Lawrence Hill & Co, Westport, USA, 1980 edition

Leo Huberman and Paul M Sweezy, *Cuba: Anatomy of a Revolution*, Modern Reader paperback, New York, 1968 edition

KS Karol, *Cuba and the USSR,* in *Cuban Communism*, edited by Irving Louis Horowitz, Transaction Books, London, 5th Edition

KS Karol, *Guerrillas in Power*, Hill and Wang, New York, 1970

Keesing's Record of World Events, Longman (to 1994), Cartermill, (1995-96), Keesing's Worldwide, (1997-)

VI Lenin, *Collected Works*, Foreign Languages Publishing House, Moscow, 1962

Doug Lorimer, *The Cuban Revolution and Its Leadership: A Criticism of Peter Taaffe's Pamphlet 'Cuba: Analysis of the Revolution* in *The Activist*, bulletin of the DSP, Vol 9, No 4, June 1999

Doug Lorimer, *Trotsky's theory of Permanent Revolution: A Leninist critique* Resistance Books, Chippendale, NSW, Australia, 1998,

John Percy, *A History of the Democratic Socialist Party – The First Two Decades*, New Course Publications, Chippendale, NSW, Australia, 1993 edition

John Reed, *Ten Days That Shook the World*, Penguin, 1977 edition

Tony Saunois, *Che Guevara, Symbol of Struggle*, CWI, 1997

Robert Scheer and Maurice Zeitlin, *Cuba: an American Tragedy*, Penguin, London, 1964

Tad Szulc, *Fidel a Critical Portrait*, Hutchinson, London, 1987

Peter Taaffe *Cuba: Analysis of the Revolution*, Militant, London, 1982 edition

Hugh Thomas, *Cuba or The Pursuit of Freedom*, Eyre and Spottiswoode, London, 1971

Leon Trotsky, *The Permanent Revolution*, Pathfinder, 1969

Leon Trotsky, *Writings of Leon Trotsky (1939-40)*, Pathfinder, 1973 edition

C Wright Mills, *Listen, Yankee: The Revolution in Cuba*, Ballentine, New York, 1960

Maurice Zeitlin, *Cuba's Workers, Workers' Cuba (1969),* new introduction to Revolutionary Politics and the Cuban Working Class, Harper, New York, 1970

Contacting the CWI

The Committee for a Workers' International has affiliated parties and organisations in more than 35 countries on all continents. The way to contact our comrades differs from country to country. Some you can contact directly. For others, it is easier to do it via the CWI offices in London... e-mail to the International Office of the CWI: inter@dircon.co.uk or contact us at PO Box 3688, London, E11 1YE, UK. Telephone: + 44 (0)20 8558 5814. Fax: + 44 (0)20 8988 8793. Our website is on: http://www.worldsocialist-cwi.org

If you want to know more about us in...Canada, Cyprus, Israel/Palestine, Italy, Pakistan, Mexico or anywhere else...then contact the CWI international offices above.

Australia: Socialist Party.
PO Box 1015, Collingwood, Victoria 3066.
phone: + 61 3 9650 0160;
e-mail: militant@mira.net
Austria: Sozialistische Linkspartie.
Kaiserstrasse 14/11, 1070 Wien. phone: + 43 1 524 6310; fax: + 43 1 524 6311;
e-mail: sov@gmx.net
Belgium: Militant Links. PB 2, 9000 Gent 21. phone: + 32 9 232 1394;
fax: + 32 9 232 1394;
e-mail: militant.links@pandora.be
Brazil: Socialismo Revolucionario. Caixa Postal 02009, CEP 01060-970, Sao Paulo S.P. phone: + 55 11 339 5684
e-mail: sr-cio@uol.com.br
Britain: Socialist Party. PO Box 24697, London, E11 1YD. phone: + 44 (0)20 8988 8777; fax: + 44 (0)20 8988 8787;
e-mail: campaigns@socialistparty.org
Canada: Socialist Resistance.
e-mail: simone@interlog.com
Chile: Celso C Campos, Casilla 50310, Correo Central, Santiago.
phone: + 56 2 622 9004
CIS: 125167 Moscow a\Ya 37, Moscow.
e-mail: pabgem@glas.apc.org
Czech Republic: Socialistická Alternativa - Budoucnost.
D.V.S., PO Box 227, Bubenské nábřeži 306, 170 05 Praha 7-Holešovice
e-mail: budoucnost@email.cz
France: Gauche Révolutionnaire - La Commune. BP 18, 93114 Rosny Cédex.
phone: + 33 (0)1 42 87 56 44;
fax: + 33 (0)1 48 57 68 62;
e-mail: grc@l-egalite.org
Germany: Sozialistische Alternative.
Litten Straße. 106/107, 10179 Berlin.
phone: + 49 302 47 23 802;
e-mail: savbund@t-online.de
Greece: Xekinima. Odos Maisonos 1, Vathis Platia, 104 38 Athens.
phone/fax: + 30 1 524 7177;
e-mail: xekinima@ath.forthnet.gr

India: Dudiyora Horaata.
PO Box 1828, Bangalore 560018.
e-mail: admin@horata.ilban.ernet.in
Ireland North: Socialist Party.
2nd Floor, 36 Victoria Square, Belfast BT1.
phone: + 44 (0)2890 232962;
fax: + 44 (0)2890 311778;
e-mail: socialist@belfastsp.freeserve.co.uk
Ireland South: Socialist Party.
PO Box 3434, Dublin 8. phone/fax: + 353 1 677 25 92; e-mail: dublinsp@clubi.ie
Israel/Palestine: Maavak Sozialisti.
e-mail: info@maavak.org.il
Japan: CWI Japan. Urbain Higashi Mikuni 9-406, Higashi-Mikuni 2-10, Yadokawa–ku, Osaka-shi. phone/fax: + 81 6 396 6998; e-mail: ni&sc@gaia-net.or.jp
Netherlands: Offensief.
PO Box 11561, 1001 GN Amsterdam.
e-mail: offensief@offensief.demon.nl
Nigeria: Democratic Socialist Movement.
PO Box 2225, Agege, Lagos.
tel: +234 1492 5671
e-mail: dsm@beta.linkserve.com
Portugal: Alternativa Socialista.
Apartado 27018, 1201-950, Lisboa
e-mail: alternativa_socialista@hotmail.com
Scotland: CWI Scotland. 5th Floor, 73 Robertson Street, Glasgow, G2 8QD.
phone: + 44 141 221 7714;
South Africa: Democratic Socialist Movement. PO Box 596, Newton, 2113, Johannesburg. phone: + 27 11 342 2220;
e-mail: democraticsocialist@mweb.co.za
Spain: Manifiesto.
Apd. de correos 4435, CP41001, Sevilla
Sri Lanka: United Socialist Party.
261/1 Kirula Road, Narahempito, Colombo 5. phone: + 94 1 508 821
Sweden: Rattvisepartiet Socialisterna;
Box 374; S- 123 03 Farsta. phone: + 46 8 605 9400. fax: + 46 8 556 252 52;
e-mail: rs@socialisterna.org
USA: Socialist Alternative - Justice.
3311 Mission Street, Suite 135, San Francisco, California 94110.

Other Publications

Other publications from the CWI include:

Che Guevara: Symbol of Struggle by Tony Saunois
£2.00 + 40p (postage & packing)

Uprising in Albania by Lynn Walsh
£1.50 + 40p (postage & packing)
No to Maastricht: No to a Bosses Europe - Fight for a Socialist Europe
(in five languages) *£1.50 + 40p (postage & packing)*
South Korea: The Tiger Strikes by Ann Cook
£1.50 + 40p (postage & packing)
The Future for Socialism (CWI/CIO European School 1996 Reports)
£1.50 + 40p (postage & packing)
Indonesia: An Unfinished Revolution by Ann Cook
£1.50 + 40p (postage & packing)
Global Turmoil: Capitalist Crisis - A Socialist Alternative
£5.00 + 40p (postage & packing)

All these pamphlets are available from
CWI Publications,
PO Box 3688, London, E11 1YE, Britain
Telephone: ++44 (0)20 8558 5814
Fax: ++44 (0)20 8788 8793
Special Offer: 5 pamphlets for £5.00 (postage free)